ULTIMATE GUIDE TO
FOOTBALL

D0003271

By James Buckley, Jr.

Produced by Shoreline Publishing Group LLC

Santa Barbara, California
www.shorelinepublishing.com
President/Editorial Director: James Buckley, Jr.
Designed by Tom Carling, www.carlingdesign.com
Illustrations by Mike Arnold, www.arnomation.com
Thanks and a tip o' the football helmet to NFL experts Jim Gigliotti and Matt Marini.

Photo Credits: All photos courtesy of Focus on Football except the following:
AP/Wide World: 19, 21, 36, 63, 69, 71, 83, 104 (2), 110, 111, 123, 126, 127, 131, 134, 135, 145
Motoring Picture Library: 11

Thanks to Jackie Carter, Marie O'Neill, Elizabeth Ward, Janet Castiglione, and Geoff Smith
in the Scholastic Library Group for championing this book and making sure that everyone else
liked it, too!

Library of Congress Cataloging-in-Publication Data

Buckley, James, 1963–
  Scholastic ultimate guide to football / by James Buckley Jr.
    p. cm.–(Scholastic ultimate guides)
  Includes bibliographical references and index.
  ISBN-13: 978-0-531-20752-9 (lib. bdg.) 978-0-531-21023-9 (pbk.)
  ISBN-10: 0-531-20752-8 (lib. bdg.) 0-531-21023-5 (pbk.)
  1. National Football League–Juvenile literature. 2. Football–United States–Juvenile literature.
    I. Scholastic Inc. II. Title. III. Title: Scholastic ultimate guide to football.
  GV955.5.N35B88 2009
  796.332'64–dc22
                                2009011003

1 2 3 4 5 6 7 8 9 10 R 19 18 17 16 15 14 13 12 11 10   Printed in the United States.

INTRODUCTION

trap yourself into a comfortable chair and let's *read* football! Okay, that doesn't sound like as much fun as "Strap on your pads and let's *play* some football!" but you can't play football at night and, you know, sometimes the weather is bad. And then there are days you just feel like lying around reading. Thank goodness that you've got the ***Scholastic Ultimate Guide to Football*** to enjoy!

This book covers the National Football League from top to bottom, beginning to end, inside and outside. We guarantee that your favorite team is in here . . . of course, that's because we gave each team its own two-page section. You'll also find lots of other cool stuff we think you'll like, from Super Bowl heroes to bizarre nicknames. Learn who The Stork was and why a snot-bubbler is as gross as its sounds. Take a trip back to football's earliest days, plus revisit the most recent Super Bowl heroics.

Football's a fun game to play, but even if you can't get out and play, it's a fun game to watch or read about. Enjoy this *ultimate guide* to the game. And when the rain lets up, go outside and play it!

CONTENTS

KICKOFF!

Every NFL game starts with a kickoff . . . and so does this book! This chapter takes a short trip back in time to set the stage for the game today. Find out how Teddy Roosevelt saved football . . . how Jim Thorpe helped start the NFL . . . and just who was the Galloping Ghost! Pro football has changed a lot from then until now. Knowing where it came from will help you enjoy it today. Let's play football! (But if you are going to play now, put the book down first . . . we don't want to get it all muddy!)

INSIDE:

Adam Vinatieri of the Colts kicks off our book!

FOOTBALL

People have been kicking things since the first caveman stubbed his toe on a rock. They've been tossing things since then, too. (The caveman stubbed his toe, bent down, and picked up the rock to throw at a passing mastodon.) Pretty soon, all that kicking and throwing turned into games. Let's take a look at how football got from there to here. (Note: No cavemen were harmed in the making of this book.)

KISS THE PIG!

In England in the Middle Ages, someone figured out that if you filled the bladder from a pig with air, it would make a nifty ball. (No word on who had to put his lips on a pig bladder . . . yuck!) Folks would then kick, carry, throw, and punch the ball all over the place.

A REALLY BIG FIELD

One type of game pitted village against village on a field that was miles long. A smaller version of what is known as "Shrovetide Football" is still played in England once a year.

FINALLY . . . THE FIRST GAME

In 1869, guys from Princeton and Rutgers colleges got together and played a "football" game. It was more like a combination of rugby and pro wrestling than football, but everyone calls it the "first football game." Rutgers won 6–4.

PUDGE GOES PRO

Colleges had the first football teams. Soon, athletic clubs had teams, too—and they all wanted the best players. In 1892, William "Pudge" Heffelfinger got $500 from a Pennsylvania club, making him the official "first pro player." Today's NFL players should say, "Thank you, Pudge!"

THINGS GET UGLY

Football in those early days was rough. Passing was illegal at first. Every play was a pile of guys smashing together—"three yards and a cloud of dust." In fact, in 1905, 18 men were actually killed while playing. Something had to change or football would disappear.

KICKS OFF!

THANKS, TED!

Riding to the rescue was the Old Rough Rider himself, President Theodore Roosevelt, a big sports fan. In late 1905, he called a meeting of football schools. He told them to stop the violence or he'd ban the sport.

NEW RULES

In 1906, the forward pass was made legal. Teams needed ten yards for a first down, not five. Games were shortened to 60 minutes. The game quickly got better, more fun, and safer. Looks like football will stick around for a while.

Is President Roosevelt signaling a touchdown?

THINGS FROM EARLY FOOTBALL THAT YOU DON'T SEE TODAY

◎ **THE FLYING WEDGE:** Ten blockers form a triangle, or wedge. The 11th player carries the ball behind the wedge. People get run over and hurt. Touchdown! The play was made illegal in 1906.

◎ **THE JUMP-PASS:** Until 1933, the passer had to be five yards behind the line of scrimmage. Some players faked a run and then stopped and jumped up to pass the ball. The passes never went very far, so no one really tries that anymore (on purpose!).

◎ **THE DROPKICK:** Before passing came along, footballs were rounder at the ends. They bounced more easily, too. Players could drop the ball on its end and kick it the instant it hit the ground. They could make field goals and extra points this way. Dropkicks are still legal, but only Doug Flutie of the Patriots in 2005 has tried and made one in the past 65 years.

CONGRATULATIONS

By the end of World War I in 1918, several dozen clubs were playing pro football. But they kept stealing players from each other. That made it difficult for any team to earn money. Time to get organized! In 1920 in Canton, Ohio, the leaders of some of the biggest teams got together and formed the American

THEN

▶ Of the 14 teams, nine were from Ohio or Illinois.

▶ One of the teams in 1920 was the Cardinals.*

▶ No team west of Illinois.

▶ By 1925, teams included the Bears, Giants, and Packers.

▶ 1932 rushing champ (first official): Cliff Battles, 576 yards.

▶ Average player's salary: about $100/game.

▶ Typical ticket price: $1.

▶ Cheerleaders? No.

▶ Instant replay? No! They didn't even have TV!

NFL FIRST FACTS

• The league's **first** president was Jim Thorpe. That's right, the famous Olympic athlete. He was also one of the best players in early pro football. Take that, Tom Brady! • The **first** game was between Dayton and Columbus. • Lou Partlow scored the **first** NFL touchdown for Dayton, which won 14–0. • The **first** NFL champion was the Akron Pros, who went 8–0–3. • Fritz Pollard, the league's **first** African American coach, led the Pros to the title. • The **first** night game was played in 1929, when the host Providence Steam Roller beat the Cardinals 16–0.

*The Cardinals are the oldest team in professional football, with a history that goes all the way back to 1898! In 1920, the team was in Chicago. The Cardinals play in Arizona now.

. IT'S A LEAGUE!

Professional Football Association (APFA). That's what it was called until 1922, when it was renamed the National Football League. Today, the NFL is made up of the National Football Conference (NFC) and the American Football Conference (AFC). Here are some of the differences between then and now.

NOW

▶ Of the 32 teams, only three are from Ohio or Illinois.

▶ One of the teams in 2009 was the Cardinals, too.

▶ 11 teams west of Illinois.

▶ Hey, look: 2009 has Bears, Giants, and Packers, too!

▶ 2008 rushing champ: Adrian Peterson, Minnesota, 1,760 yards.

▶ Average player's salary: $100,000/game.

▶ Typical ticket price: $72.

▶ Cheerleaders? Yes.

▶ Instant replay? Yes.

HUT, HUT, HUPMOBILE!

Why is the Hupmobile a part of NFL history? And what the heck is a Hupmobile? It was a type of car, like a Ford or a Toyota. The meeting of team owners that led to the creation of the NFL was held in a Hupmobile store. You won't see many Hupmobiles today—the company went out of business in 1940.

THE INDOOR GAME

Football is a game meant to be played outdoors, in the mud, dirt, snow, ice, and, well . . . more mud. But it was one indoor game that had the biggest impact on pro football in its first three decades. Following—and thanks to—this game, many new rules were put in place that changed the face of football.

The Set-Up

The Chicago Bears and the Portsmouth Spartans finished the 1932 season pretty much tied. There was no official playoff system, but everyone wanted to know who the champ was. The league decided to have the two teams play each other. The winner would be the NFL champ.

The Place

A terrible blizzard closed Chicago's outdoor Wrigley Field. A circus had just closed up shop at the indoor Chicago Arena. Bingo! The NFL moved indoors. One problem: There was only room for an 80-yard field!

The Game

The Bears won 9–0, thanks to a touchdown pass from Bronko Nagurski to Red Grange. Big issue: Was Nagurski at least five yards behind the line of scrimmage when he threw the pass? That was the rule at the time. The refs said yes, but Portsmouth fans complained. And so . . .

The Changes

☑ Passing was made legal from anywhere behind the line of scrimmage. Suddenly, being a quarterback became a pretty cool thing.

☑ Hash marks were made a regular part of the NFL field. If a play ended outside the hash marks, the next play would start at the hash mark, not right next to the sideline, as it had before. This gave the offense space to run plays to either side of the field.

☑ Goalposts were moved to the goal line; they would move back to the end line again in 1974.

☑ Playoffs were officially started. The winners of each of the two NFL divisions would play each other for the NFL title.

THE SNEAKERS
GAME

Another game from the early days of the NFL lives on, thanks to the players' feet. No, it was not the day that NFL players were the stinkiest. Trust us, we do NOT want to be the judge of that contest. We're talking about the 1934 NFL Championship Game . . . and the freezing New York City weather that made it famous.

Here's how we imagine the conversation went early in the game, with the Giants trailing on an icy field.

Player: I feel like I'm on ice skates out there. My cleats won't dig in!

Coach: How do you think I feel? At least you get to run around!

Player: Seriously, Coach, what are we gonna do?

Equipment manager: Um, guys? Why don't we switch to sneakers?

(Coach and player stare at tiny equipment guy . . . then at each other.)

Player and Coach: GO!

(Equipment manager leaves stadium, tries several stores, but all are closed on Sunday. Finally finds big batch at Manhattan College gym. Arrives back at halftime with basketball shoes for all the players.)

Player (trying on sneakers): This is great! I can run!

Coach: Okay, go, boys, go!

The Giants' new shoes gripped the ice like glue. The Bears kept sliding around in their cleats. Guess who won? That's right, the Sneaky Giants, 30–13, over the Slip-Slidy Bears.

THE
GALLOPING GHOST

"Red" Grange

Harold "Red" Grange
Chicago Bears Halfback

BORN: June 13, 1903 • HT.: 6-0 WT.: 180
COLLEGE: University of Illinois

The man known as the "Galloping Ghost" burst onto the college football scene as a superstar at the University of Illinois. He was the most famous football player in the country. He signed with the Chicago Bears in 1925. Nearly 70,000 people packed a stadium to see him; a month earlier, the Bears had attracted only 4,000 fans.

Grange went on a national tour, filling seats and raking in ticket money as he went. The attention Grange got made the NFL famous for the first time. Some say that without The Ghost, the NFL would have faded away. With him, it continued its march to greatness.

Career Scoring Totals

Rushing Touchdowns	21
Touchdown Passes	10
Touchdown Receptions	10

THE MIGHTY
PACKERS

The Green Bay Packers joined the NFL in 1921. They almost folded a couple of years later. But a brilliant idea saved them: Fans chipped in money to buy shares in the team. Bingo! The team was saved. It is still owned collectively by its fans.

The Packers soon rewarded their fans with a trio of championships. They won each of them in slightly different ways. Here's how they became the first team to win three straight NFL titles.

1929 The Packers defense allowed only 22 points in 13 games! That's fewer than two points per game! They beat the Giants 20–6, handing the Giants their only defeat. The Packers' 12–0–1 record made them league champs for the first time.

1930 Though passing was legal, few teams did it very often. Arnie Herber, the new Packers quarterback, changed that. His long touchdown passes propelled the Packers to their second title. Herber's favorite target was Johnny "Blood" McNally, who took his "football name" from a silent movie.

1931 The Packers won their first title with defense. They won their third straight with a dominant offense. They led the league with 291 points. With Herber out with an injury, his replacement, Red Dunn, led the NFL with eight touchdown passes. McNally starred again, too.

WHAT THEY WORE

Football players in the sport's early days had hard heads. Or we hope they did, because they didn't wear helmets! Well, at least at first they didn't. Some players started using hard leather helmets in the early 1900s, but many still chose to play bareheaded. The helmets didn't have facemasks, either. Here's a look at what a typical football player wore until plastics were improved during World War II, making gear safer, lighter, and easier to clean.

HELMET Hard leather, no facemask. Chin strap went under chin, not on it.

JERSEY Heavy wool, with light leather or cloth pads sewn into shoulders.

PANTS Heavy canvas to just below the knees. Some players sewed in leather or cloth pads at the hips and knees.

SHOES High-top leather cleats. The cleats were metal or heavy leather and much longer than those that today's players use.

OTHER PADS Uh . . . none. No mouthguard, no shin guards, no large shoulder pads, no flak jackets, no tailbone pads, no neck collars . . . no cups.

ON THE NOSE

One way players tried to protect their schnozzes was with this leather noseguard. A strap went around the player's head. He held the bottom part in his teeth. One problem: When opponents grabbed the noseguard . . . the teeth sometimes came with it. Noseguards were not used for very long (and many dentists cried).

FUNKY AND DEFUNCT
TEAMS THAT DISAPPEARED

Quiz time! Below is a list of football teams. Ten of them were real teams during the league's early years, when teams started and folded often. Two of them are just silly names we made up. Can you find the fakes? Answers at the bottom.

Columbus Panhandles
Dayton Triangles
Duluth Kelleys
Evansville Crimson Giants
Joliet Jumping Beans
Kansas City Cowboys
Massillon Maulers
Oorang Indians
Orange Tornadoes
Providence Steam Roller
Racine Tornadoes
Staten Island Stapletons

ANSWER: The fake NFL teams are the Joliet Jumping Beans and the Massillon Maulers.

THE GREATEST

Through the 2008 season, the NFL has played about 13,000 games. Some were boring, some were good, some were great. But of all those games, just one is known as "The Greatest Game Ever Played." So, what made the 1958 NFL Championship Game between the Baltimore Colts and the New York Giants so great? Let us count the ways:

10 Yankee Stadium A baseball field? That's right, the greatest NFL game ever was played on the infield and outfield usually used by the legendary New York Yankees.

9 Weather As with all classic football games, this one was played in the cold. Fans and players alike bundled up to battle the chill of a late December afternoon.

8 Bravery With just moments to go in the game, Baltimore defensive end Gino Marchetti broke his leg. He wouldn't let medical personnel carry him to an ambulance, though. He sat on his stretcher to watch the end of the game.

7 Money, money Each player on the winning team (the Colts) was paid almost $5,000. That was about half of most players' yearly salaries. (By 2008, players earned $78,000 for winning a Super Bowl.)

These men all took part in the 1958 championship game. Later, they were elected to the Pro Football Hall of Fame, located in Canton, Ohio, site of the meetings that formed the NFL. With this lineup, no wonder it was "the greatest game ever played"!

NEXT STOP:

CANTON, OHIO!

COLTS WR Raymond Berry, DT Art Donovan, Coach Weeb Ewbank, DE Gino Marchetti, RB Lenny Moore, T Jim Parker, QB Johnny Unitas

GIANTS T Roosevelt Brown, RB Frank Gifford, LB Sam Huff, Coach Tom Landry, Coach Vince Lombardi, Owner Tim Mara, Owner Wellington Mara, WR Don Maynard, DE Andy Robustelli, S Emlen Tunnell

GAME EVER PLAYED

6 Hall of Famers An awesome 17 people connected to the game are now in the Hall of Fame (see box).

5 Johnny Unitas The man who many experts call the greatest quarterback ever was at his finest in this game. He called all the plays, made the throws, and took the hits. In this game, he also pretty much invented . . .

4 . . . the two-minute drill Every quarterback can run this late-game hurry-up offense now, but it was rare then. Unitas drove the Colts downfield in the last minutes of regulation time to set up a game-tying field goal. Then in overtime, he led them to the winning touchdown.

3 Overtime game What's that? Overtime? This was the first (and still only) NFL title game to be decided by sudden-death overtime. Some players didn't even know that they would keep playing after 60 minutes was up and the score was 17–17.

2 Famous photo One of the most famous sports photos ever shows Colts running back Alan "The Horse" Ameche bulling into the end zone for the winning score (on TV above).

1 TV! Okay, those are all nice reasons. But the No. 1 reason the game is called "the greatest" was that a record-breaking audience of more than 45 million people watched the game on national TV. They saw an exciting, back-and-forth, overtime classic. Today, thanks to TV, the NFL is America's most popular sport. And the connection between the league and TV pretty much started with this game.

BUFFALO BILLS

Buffalo fans might win the award for toughest in the league. They brave freezing cold, snow, ice, and sleet to cheer for their team. Although the Bills are still looking for their first Super Bowl title, their fans remain loyal!

GAME 1?
1960

The Bills were among the ten original members of the American Football League (AFL), which started in 1960. In 1970, the AFL merged with the NFL, and the Bills joined the new AFC.

 ## MAGIC MOMENT
No. 1 Comeback!

Buffalo trailed the Houston Oilers 35–3 in a 1992 playoff game. The Bills roared back to tie the score and then won in overtime!

 ## LOWEST LOW
Super Bowl XXV

A 47-yard field goal would have given the Bills the Super Bowl title, but it sailed wide right, and they lost to the Giants 20–19.

STUFF

HOME:
Ralph Wilson Stadium

SUPER BOWL TITLES: **0**

ONLY IN BUFFALO:
A man named "Pinto Ron" cooks a huge pre-game barbecue for fans on the hood of his 1980 Ford Pinto.

STAR SEASONS!

1964 The Bills won 12 regular-season games, then beat San Diego for their first AFL championship.

1990 Buffalo swamped the Los Angeles Raiders 51–3 to win its first AFC championship.

1993 Wrapping up one of the most dominant periods in league history, the Bills captured their sixth straight division crown and fourth straight AFC title.

The Ultimate Bill
JIM KELLY

The master of the no-huddle "K-Gun" offense led the Bills to four straight AFC championships (1990–1993). No other team has matched that record! Kelly's powerful arm and famous toughness made him an all-around great. His leadership helped the Bills bounce back from some tough losses, too.

#1

FUNKY FACTS

→ Bad luck played a part in the Bills' four Super Bowl losses. For instance, just before the start of Super Bowl XXVI, someone moved star running back Thurman Thomas's helmet and he had to miss the game's first plays!

→ Every kicker in the NFL kicks soccer-style today, but the first to do it was Buffalo's Pete Gogolak in 1964. Before him, kickers booted the ball with their toes!

→ Talk about getting off on the wrong foot. When Buffalo opened its new stadium in 1973, the visiting Washington Redskins ran back the opening kickoff for a touchdown!

SUPERSTAR!
LEE EVANS

The Bills can depend on steady production from this wide receiver. Evans has topped 1,000 yards in a season twice and has been the team's receptions leader since 2006.

→ The extra padding that safety Mark Kelso wore on his helmet made him look like The Great Gazoo from the comics.

You Can Look It Up! BUFFALO'S OFFICIAL WEBSITE: www.buffalobills.com

MIAMI
DOLPHINS

The Dolphins can look back with pride at the greatest season in NFL history. But they have to look a looong way back! With some magical names in their past, the "Fish" (we know . . . dolphins aren't fish) swim into the future.

GAME 1?
1966

The Dolphins were the first expansion team to join the AFL. They played their first game in 1966, and lost to the Oakland Raiders. They joined the NFL with other AFL teams in 1970.

 ## MAGIC MOMENT
Super Bowl VII

With a 14–7 Super Bowl win over the Redskins, the Dolphins completed the only undefeated season in NFL history, finishing 17–0.

 ## LOWEST LOW
The 2007 season

Throw this one back in the Atlantic Ocean. The Dolphins lost 13 straight before winning one. They finished an ugly 1–15.

STUFF

HOME:
Dolphin Stadium

SUPER BOWL TITLES: **2**

ONLY IN MIAMI:
After every touchdown, the team plays its fight song. It was first played during the magical and "perfect" 1972 season.

STAR SEASONS!

1973
The Dolphins became the second team to capture back-to-back Super Bowl titles.

1984
Dan Marino set all sorts of records, and the Dolphins earned a trip to the Super Bowl.

2008
After winning only one game the season before, the Dolphins (11–5) became the first team to reach the playoffs a year after such a disaster!

The Ultimate Dolphin
DAN MARINO

When Marino retired after the 1999 season, he was the NFL's (and the Dolphins', of course) all-time leader in pass attempts, completions, touchdowns, and yards. Brett Favre has since knocked him off the top spots, but the rocket-armed Marino remains No. 1 in Miami fans' hearts.

FUNKY FACTS

→ The Dolphins were not the first pro team in Miami. In 1946, the Miami Seahawks played one season in the short-lived All-America Football Conference.

→ The Dolphins found themselves without several star players in 1974 when they "jumped" to the World Football League, a new pro outfit. It only lasted a couple of years, though. And the NFL ruled again!

→ Coach Don Shula led the Dolphins from 1970–1985. He earned 247 of his all-time record of 347 wins while with the Dolphins.

→ Another nickname for the Miami team: Just call them "The Fins."

SUPERSTAR!
RONNIE BROWN

The rumbling running of Ronnie Brown played a big part in the Dolphins' amazing 2008 season. He led the Fins with ten touchdowns and powered their solid rushing attack.

→ The 1994 movie *Ace Ventura: Pet Detective* shows a live dolphin swimming at Dolphin Stadium. But that was total fiction!

You Can Look It Up! MIAMI'S OFFICIAL WEBSITE: www.miamidolphins.com

NEW ENGLAND
PATRIOTS

The Patriots came close to winning it all a couple of times, but they always fell short. But then along came Brady . . . and wily coach Bill Belichick. With three Super Bowl wins and four AFC titles in the past decade, they're a dynasty!

GAME 1?
1960

The Boston Patriots were part of the new American Football League (AFL) when that league kicked off in 1960. In 1971, they changed their name to the New England Patriots.

MAGIC MOMENT
Super Bowl XXXVIII

Tied with Carolina at 29–29, the Patriots called on kicker Adam Vinatieri. His kick with four seconds left was good—the Pats won!

LOWEST LOW
Super Bowl XLII

Less than a minute away from earning the NFL's first 19–0 record, the Patriots lost, thanks to the Giants' miracle finish.

STUFF

HOME:
Gillette Stadium

SUPER BOWL TITLES: **3**

ONLY IN NEW ENGLAND:
A man in New Hampshire had his bald head tattooed to look just like a Patriots helmet!

STAR SEASONS!

1985 The Patriots won their first AFC championship. They got mauled by the Chicago Bears in the Super Bowl, however.

2001 A miracle playoff win over Oakland led to the Patriots' first Super Bowl championship. They won by beating the Rams.

2007 The Patriots became the first team since the 1972 Dolphins to win every regular-season game.

The Ultimate Patriot
TOM BRADY

He was a sixth-round draft pick. He only got the job when Drew Bledsoe got injured. But he stepped in and became a legend. Brady led the Pats to three Super Bowl titles in four seasons (2001–2004), earning two Super Bowl MVP trophies. Look for Brady to take his place among the all-time greats.

FUNKY FACTS

→ Baseball or football? From 1963–1970, the Patriots played their home games at Fenway Park, which is better known for the Boston Red Sox and the towering Green Monster!

→ The Patriots won a 1982 game 3–0, thanks to a snowplow driver. Without asking permission, he drove onto the field to clear a small spot on the snow-covered turf for kicker John Smith, who made a field goal for the game's only points!

→ Oops! In 2007, coach Bill Belichick was fined $500,000 for secretly taping and stealing other teams' signals. Naughty coach!

SUPERSTAR!
TOM BRADY

It's that man again! Brady set an NFL record in 2007 by throwing an amazing 50 touchdown passes. He missed 2008 with an injury but expects to be back on the field ready to keep winning.

→ The original Patriots logo was nicknamed "Pat Patriot." In 1993, they changed to their current look. But fans missed Pat and called the new logo "The Flying Elvis."

You Can Look It Up! NEW ENGLAND'S OFFICIAL WEBSITE: www.patriots.com

NEW YORK JETS

Though they're often lost in the shadow of the New York Giants, with whom they share a stadium, the Jets have their own devoted fans. The team has had one amazing highlight, and Jets lovers await another one . . . soon!

GAME 1?
1960

The New York Titans played their first game in 1960 as part of the new AFL. In 1963, the team changed its name to the New York Jets. They joined the NFL with other AFL teams in 1970.

 ## MAGIC MOMENT
Super Bowl III

Joe Namath guaranteed that his Jets would upset the favored Colts. Namath made his bold words stand up, and the Jets won!

 ## LOWEST LOW
A One-Win Season

The Jets suffered through their worst season ever in 1996, finishing 1–15. They threw more interceptions than touchdowns!

STUFF

HOME:
Giants Stadium

SUPER BOWL TITLES: **1**

ONLY IN NEW JERSEY:
A longtime fan named "Fireman Ed" rides another fan's shoulders to lead a famous cheer: "J-E-T-S, Jets, Jets, Jets!"

STAR SEASONS!

1968 The Jets surprised many by beating Oakland to win the AFL title. Then they surprised EVERYONE by winning the Super Bowl, too.

1984 Mark Gastineau set a record (since broken) with 22 sacks.

1998 The Jets set a team record with 12 wins, won the AFC East, and earned a spot in their second AFC Championship Game.

The Ultimate Jet
DON MAYNARD

Surprise! It's not Joe Namath. He's close, but we'll go with this Hall of Fame receiver, who played for the team for its first 13 seasons. Maynard still holds the Jets record with 88 TD catches. Not the biggest guy around, he was a tough guy from Texas who took the hardest hits and bounced back up.

FUNKY FACTS

➜ The Jets took part in the first Monday Night Football game ever, in 1970. They lost to the Cleveland Browns 31–21.

➜ The Heidi Game: The Jets were leading Oakland in a 1968 game with two minutes left. The TV network cut to a movie called *Heidi*. Fans at home missed the Raiders' amazing comeback victory!

➜ One of the Jets' nicknames is "Gang Green," after their uniform color. Of course, that's kind of gross, because gangrene is a nasty illness caused by dirt getting into open wounds!

SUPERSTAR!
THOMAS JONES

Jones played for three other teams before busting out with the Jets in 2008, his second year in green and white. That year, he was one of the league leaders with 15 touchdowns. He topped 1,000 yards for the fourth time.

➜ The coach who led the Jets to their Super Bowl III win was named Weeb Ewbank. We just like writing "Weeb."

You Can Look It Up! THE JETS' OFFICIAL WEBSITE: www.newyorkjets.com

FIRST
QUARTER

Let's get ready to play. In this chapter, find out how to join an NFL team, what NFL teams do to get ready for the season (and why they need so many strawberries), what gear the players need to survive . . . er, play, how coaches get their players psyched, and what all those other people running around the field do. Think of this as the chapter where you get out all the snacks before you sit down to watch the game!

INSIDE:

Aaron Rodgers to the Packers: "Everybody go long!"

DO YOU FEEL

How can you get a job as an NFL player? Well, assuming you're amazingly talented, big, fast, strong, dedicated, and all that . . . your first stop is probably the NFL Draft. Since 1936, NFL teams have met each spring to choose college players for their teams. The draft is designed to keep the strongest teams from grabbing all the best players. NFL teams take turns choosing players. The worst teams from the previous year go first; the Super Bowl champ picks last. Sounds fair, right?

In the past decade, Draft Day has become a spectacle. Every minute is on TV. Magazines, websites, and TV shows analyze, predict, and ponder every possible permutation (that means possibility) of the draft. Here are some facts about this amazing day.

THE BASICS

WHAT: NFL Annual Selection Draft

WHEN: In recent years, late April

WHERE: In 2009, Radio City Music Hall, New York City

WHO: At least 224 college players are chosen by 32 teams in seven rounds

THE FIRST

The first player chosen in the first NFL Draft was Jay Berwanger of the University of Chicago. Berwanger was chosen by the Eagles, but he decided that the NFL was no place for him. He went into business and never played pro football!

Gee, Quarterbacks Come First . . . *BIG* Surprise!

These positions have been drafted No. 1 overall in the NFL and AFL drafts since 1936.*

Quarterbacks: **28** ▶ Running backs: **23** ▶ Defensive tackles/ends: **13**

*Through 2009.

A DRAFT???

What Are **"DRAFTNIKS"?**

The silly answer is "people without a life." The real answer is fans who are *obsessed* with the NFL Draft. They follow each round, pick by pick. They track the players, cheer their favorites, and boo at picks they consider bad. The draft site is packed with these fans, many dressed in team jerseys. (*P.S.: Okay . . . we admit it—we've been to the draft and done all that. Sorry.*)

MR. IRRELEVANT

Being picked in the first or second round is a pretty good sign that you're on your way to a nice NFL career. Being picked in later rounds means you're probably a pretty good player but maybe not a superstar.

Being picked last in the NFL Draft, however, is not like being picked last in dodgeball. You're still on your way to the NFL! You're also on your way to Newport Beach, California, which celebrates the last pick as "Mr. Irrelevant." That means someone who just doesn't matter. Newport Beach decided to make the last pick *matter* by giving him a parade and other honors.

TIME FOR CAMP!

Camp is fun, right? Summer weather, good friends, canoeing, bunk beds, campfires . . . the whole nine yards. Guess what? Football players **hate** going to camp. Teams' training camps start in the summer, but they're anything but fun. NFL teams gather up their players to prepare for the new season. For many players, it's their only chance to impress the coaches and earn a spot on the roster.

The players gather at a team camp, where they stay full-time for weeks. They practice (sometimes twice a day), eat together, go to meeting after meeting, and work their tails off. No s'mores for them! Here's a look at some of the facts and stories about training camp.

SING, ROOKIE!

Rookie players at their first NFL training camp need to come prepared. Not with football gear—with a song! During the first week of camp, older players force the rookies to sing their college fight songs in front of the whole team. Trust us: Linebackers make better tacklers than singers.

Typical Daily Schedule

Keep those alarm clocks handy!
Here's a typical day at an NFL training camp:

7 a.m.	Breakfast
8 a.m.	Team meeting
9-11:30 a.m.	First practice session
11:30-2 p.m.	Lunch break
2 p.m.	Watch film with position groups (receivers, linebackers, etc.)
3:30-5:30 p.m.	Second practice session
6-7 p.m.	Dinner
8-9:30 p.m.	Meetings or more film study
10 p.m.	Snack time
11 p.m.	Lights out!

ONE TEAM'S MENU

Put 60 or 70 giant human beings in one place and make them work and work . . . and you'll need a lot of food to keep them going. Here's what one team ate in only three weeks during one of its training camps:

13,000 strawberries

5,000 eggs

4,500 chicken breasts

3,600 bananas

3,200 steaks

1,500 waffles

1,200 bowls of soup

600 whole chickens

Who Is **The Turk**?

The worst words that a player can hear at training camp are "Coach would like to see you. Bring your playbook." That means only one thing: The player has been cut and he's going home. The unlucky person who brings this news is known as "The Turk." Saying that "The Turk came to see me" is all you'll have to say to your teammates before you leave.

GEARING UP

What does the modern, well-dressed NFL player wear during games? Let's take a stroll over to the football fashion (and protection) runway and check it out. Our model is the always-stylish quarterback Matt Ryan of the Atlanta Falcons.

A: Starting at the top, it's the helmet! It's made of high-impact plastic. The inside is filled with pads and small air bags. Each player has his helmet specially fitted to his head.

B: Facemasks are made of rubber-covered steel. They can be unscrewed and replaced if they break. They come in a variety of patterns. Some players wear clear-plastic face shields, too.

C: Stylish and sleek, the NFL jersey is made of heavy-duty nylon. Players can move and stretch and keep cool! Look for extra-tight jerseys on linemen–that's less fabric for their opponents to grab!

D: Like many QBs and some LBs, Matt wears a wristband that has a built-in card listing his team's key plays and signals. It's sort of like a cheat sheet for the huddle!

E: Thigh pads, slipped in beneath pants.

F: Pants, made of stretchy nylon, must cover the bottom of the knee.

G: Knee pads.

H: Matt, like some players, wears a metal-and-plastic knee brace under his pants for extra support.

I: Socks in the NFL must cover the entire calf; no skin-showing allowed!

J: Cleats: Most players wear ankle-covering models like these. They switch shoes for grass or artificial turf.

A (WEIRD) WORD
FROM THE COACH

Coaches have very stressful jobs. They have to manage 50-plus players, plus a staff of assistants, trainers, and other workers. They have to know all the rules, deal with the media, and keep the team owner happy. No wonder every coach from the Pop Warner league on up dreams of having one of the 32 NFL jobs!

Sometimes, all that pressure can make coaches do or say goofy things. Here are a few examples of coaches who must have been thinking, "I should have stayed a high school coach . . ."

Bill Belichick, Patriots: Fined $500,000 by the NFL for using video cameras to spy on opponents' defensive signals during games.

Jim Mora, Colts: When asked by a reporter whether he was worried about the playoffs, he screamed, "Playoffs? Playoffs?! Don't talk about playoffs! I just hope we can win a game!"

Mike Tice, Vikings: Fined $100,000 for illegally selling Super Bowl tickets. Note: Minnesota was not in the game!

Mike Singletary, 49ers (above): After he kicked tight end Vernon Davis off the bench, he said, "I told him he'd do a better job for us taking a shower and watching than playing the game."

Jim Haslett, Rams: Went so crazy yelling and cursing at officials during a game that he was later fined $20,000 by the NFL.

HONORABLE MENTION: Woody Hayes, Ohio State University: In 1978, a player from another team made an interception and ran out of bounds near Woody. Woody punched him. Seriously. Oops!

SUPERSTITIONS

Before every game, an NFL player gets his gear and his game face on. Some players depend on superstitions to get them psyched. Here are some of the more unusual rituals and superstitions NFL players observe before every game they play:

REX GROSSMAN: Does his warmups, then showers before putting on uniform

JOHN HENDERSON: Gets slapped by an assistant trainer

PEYTON MANNING: Always reads every page of the game program

MIKE SELLERS: Does not eat the night before

MAX STARKS: Eats "Shark Bites" fruit snacks

MAURICE STOVALL: Watches a Bruce Lee movie

JASON TAYLOR: Dresses from right to left

LAWRENCE TYNES: Washes his car

BRIAN URLACHER: Eats two chocolate chip cookies

TWEEEE

LET'S MEET THE ZEBRAS!

"Hey, ref! That was a lousy call!" Have you ever yelled that at your TV? Don't feel guilty; the referee couldn't hear you. Here's a bunch of info about those guys in the black-and-white shirts who boss around men twice their size using only a whistle and a little flag!

HOW DOES REPLAY WORK?

In 1999, the NFL began its current instant replay system. Thanks to modern video technology, the referee can watch TV during the game! He's not watching cartoons, of course, but looking at video replays of disputed calls. Coaches get to challenge two plays per game. But if there are two minutes or less left in a half, a replay official above the field decides whether to review a call.

EEEEET!

Seven for Justice!

Most fans call all seven game officials "ref." Actually, only one of those guys is the referee. He's the boss of the crew of officials, and he makes all the final decisions. Here are the names of the other six positions and where those officials work:

UMPIRE: a few yards behind defensive line

HEAD LINESMAN: at one side of field, on line of scrimmage

LINE JUDGE: opposite side of field from head linesman

FIELD JUDGE: same side as line judge, about 20 yards upfield

SIDE JUDGE: same side as head linesman, about 20 yards upfield

BACK JUDGE: 25–30 yards upfield from line of scrimmage, usually near center of field

HANDS UP!

Officials use hand and arm signals to tell the crowd and both teams what the penalty or play was. Some of the classics:

Hands on hips: OFFSIDE

Push hands straight out: INTERFERENCE

Hit one arm with the other: PERSONAL FOUL

Point downfield: FIRST DOWN

Both hands overhead: TOUCHDOWN OR FIELD GOAL

REF GEAR: FLAGS AND BEANBAGS

In football's early days, referees just blew their whistles and waved their arms when there was a penalty. In the 1960s, they were throwing little white cloths. Today, when they see a penalty, officials toss bright yellow flags with a small weight on one end. If they see a turnover (fumble, interception), they drop a blue beanbag.

SIDELINE PEOPLE

This photo shows a sideline at a Carolina Panthers game. Sidelines are filled with lots more people than just players. Check out the boxes on these pages and find out about the lucky ducks who get to hang with the Panthers.

TV commercial guy: *Wearing a bright green hat and long orange mittens, he signals to the referee when it's time for a TV timeout and when the commercials are over and the game can continue.*

Cheerleaders: *All but a few NFL teams have cheerleaders. They dance and cheer most often near the end zones.*

Team bench: *Only players and team workers can enter this 40-yard area during the game. Players rest on benches at the back of this area.*

Chain crew: *Referee's assistants who hold signs and a ten-yard chain that helps keep track of down and distance.*

Reserve players: *Reserves wait in this area for their turn to enter the game. They have to pay close attention so they're ready when needed.*

Photographers: *They stand on either side of the bench area and at the back of the end zones.*

Kicking net: *The kicker stands in or near the bench area and smacks practice kicks into this net.*

Trainers work area: *When players are injured or need taping or treatment, they sit or lie on tables set up behind the team bench.*

BALTIMORE RAVENS

When you think Ravens, you think defense. Since the team entered the league, it has specialized in powerful, painful defenses. In the 2000 season, their devastating D paved the way to the team's only Super Bowl title.

GAME 1?
1996

The Cleveland Browns moved to Baltimore and became the Ravens in 1996. But the Browns' history stayed in Cleveland, so the Ravens' official history started in Baltimore. It's a bit odd.

 ## MAGIC MOMENT
Super Bowl XXXV

The Ravens D scored a touchdown and denied the New York Giants any points on offense. Baltimore won 34–7.

 ## LOWEST LOW
Weak Welcome

The Ravens' first season in their new hometown, where many were still rooting for their long-lost Colts, included only four wins.

STUFF

HOME:
M&T Bank Stadium

SUPER BOWL TITLES: **1**

ONLY IN BALTIMORE:
For a while, the Ravens had three giant bird mascots: Edgar, Allan, and Poe, named for the poet who wrote "The Raven."

STAR SEASONS!

2000 On their way to the Super Bowl, the Ravens shut out four teams and allowed only ten points or fewer in 15 games!

2003 Running back Jamal Lewis ran for 2,066 yards, the second-highest single-season total ever.

2008 Joe Flacco became the first quarterback to lead a team to two playoff-game wins in his rookie season.

The Ultimate Raven
RAY LEWIS

When Ray Lewis hits you, you hurt, your children hurt, and your dog hurts. Lewis is one of the greatest linebackers ever. Want proof? Check out his two NFL Defensive Player of the Year awards and his MVP trophy from the Ravens' Super Bowl XXXV win. A certain future Hall of Famer.

FUNKY FACTS

➜ Why Ravens? A contest was held to name the new team. The winner was inspired by a famous poem–"The Raven"–written by Edgar Allan Poe, who lived much of his life in Baltimore.

➜ Jamal Lewis had a big 2003. In a game against Cleveland, he ran for 295 yards (the second-most ever) on the way to 2,066 yards for the season (also the second-most ever).

➜ The Ravens got off to a good start in Baltimore. They won their first game there in 1996, defeating the Oakland Raiders 19–14.

SUPERSTAR!
ED REED

How good is safety Ed Reed? In 2008, he was the only unanimous choice for the NFL All-Pro team. Opponents find Reed–and throw in the other direction. Smart, fast, and tough, Reed is a game-changer.

➜ Tight end Shannon Sharpe, one of the best (and loudest) Ravens ever, scored a 96-yard TD in the 2000 AFC Championship Game. It was the longest score in NFL playoff history at the time.

You Can Look It Up! BALTIMORE'S OFFICIAL WEBSITE: www.baltimoreravens.com

CINCINNATI
BENGALS

Okay, so one of their nicknames is "The Bungles." Okay, so they have sniffed the playoffs only once since 1990. They can still boast some very exciting players and two Super Bowl trips. Take that, Cleveland!

GAME 1?
1968

The Bengals joined the AFL as an expansion team in 1968. When that league merged with the NFL, the Bengals became part of the American Football Conference (AFC).

 ## MAGIC MOMENT
The Freezer Bowl

Cincinnati won its first AFC title by surviving a wind chill of minus-59 degrees to beat San Diego in the 1981 AFC Championship Game.

 ## LOWEST LOW
So Many Choices

How about 2002? The Bengals won only two games in their sixth consecutive losing season. They didn't go above .500 until 2005.

STUFF

HOME:
Paul Brown Stadium

SUPER BOWL TITLES: **0**

ONLY IN CINCINNATI:
Cincinnati's helmets used to say "Bengals" on both sides. They added tiger stripes in 1981 . . . and went to the Super Bowl!

STAR SEASONS!

1988 Rookie running back Ickey Woods ran for a team-record 15 touchdowns. (See Funky Facts.)

1995 Receiver Carl Pickens nabbed an AFC-leading 17 touchdown catches, setting a team record.

2007 Strong-armed QB Carson Palmer threw for a team-record 4,131 yards. He also threw a record 32 TD passes in 2005.

The Ultimate Bengal

ANTHONY MUÑOZ

On the list of all-time greats on the offensive line, this gentle giant's name is near the top. Muñoz was a first-round draft pick in 1980 and quickly became a star tackle in the NFL. He made the Pro Bowl 11 times and helped the Bengals win a pair of AFC titles. Hall of Famer? Duh!

FUNKY FACTS

→ The Cincinnati Bengals were founded by a man who was already a legend. Hall of Famer Paul Brown came out of retirement to be the Bengals' first coach, owner, and general manager.

→ Hop on one leg, hop on the other, hop on the first, spike the ball. You're doing the "Ickey Shuffle," a TD-celebration dance invented in 1988 by rookie star Ickey Woods.

→ How did famous Bengals QB Norman "Boomer" Esiason get his nickname? Before he was even born, he kicked inside his mother so much, she said he was "booming."

SUPERSTAR!

CARSON PALMER

Palmer lit up scoreboards in his first several seasons, setting team records for TD passes and yards. Injuries slowed him in 2008, but look for him to keep throwing . . . often!

→ Before the 2008 season, receiver Chad Johnson changed his last name to Ochocinco, after the Spanish words for his uniform number, 85. The NFL didn't let him change his jersey until 2009, since they still had a pile of Johnson'ed gear to sell!

You Can Look It Up! CINCINNATI'S OFFICIAL WEBSITE: www.cincinnatibengals.com

CLEVELAND BROWNS

One of the NFL's legendary teams, the Browns were awesome in the 1950s, pretty good in the '60s, had a few good years in the '80s . . . but have been out of the running for a while. Their fans hope to return to the good old days!

GAME 1?
1946

The Browns played four seasons in the All-America Football Conference before that league folded. The Browns then joined the rival NFL . . . and won the title in their first year!

 ## MAGIC MOMENT
A Great Start!

Few thought the Browns could keep up with the NFL's "big boys." Bad call. Cleveland beat the Rams 30–28 to win the 1950 NFL title.

 ## LOWEST LOW
Back to Earth

After making the playoffs every year from 1985–89, the Browns crashed in 1990, winning only three of their 16 games.

STUFF

HOME:
Cleveland Browns Stadium

SUPER BOWL TITLES: 0

ONLY IN CLEVELAND:
Fans in the end zone seats sit in the "Dawg Pound." They wear rubber dog masks and throw dog biscuits.

STAR SEASONS!

1955 QB Otto Graham delayed his retirement to lead the Browns to their third NFL title in six seasons.

1963 The great Jim Brown led the NFL with 1,863 rushing yards, one of his record eight titles in that category.

1980 Quarterback Brian Sipe set all-time team records with 30 TD passes and 4,132 passing yards.

The Ultimate Brown

OTTO GRAHAM

A quarterback is supposed to lead his team to championships, right? Well, nobody did that better than Otto Graham. In ten years as Cleveland's QB (1946–1955), he led the team to ten championship games. They won seven of them, including all four AAFC titles. That's why they called him "Automatic Otto."

FUNKY FACTS

➔ Cleveland's first coach was Paul Brown. He was so famous the team was named for him.

➔ The Browns twice came *thiiis* close to a Super Bowl, losing two AFC Championship Games to Denver. In 1986, John Elway tied the game with "The Drive" and won in overtime. In 1987, "The Fumble" doomed the Browns with a minute to play.

➔ For three years, there was a Cleveland Browns organization . . . but no team. After the owner moved the team to Baltimore in 1996, the NFL ruled that he couldn't take the Browns history with him. So he named his

SUPERSTAR!
BRAYLON EDWARDS

This tall, speedy receiver burst onto the NFL scene in 2007. He caught 16 touchdowns and was among the league leaders in receiving yards. He dipped a bit in 2008, but he has the skills to help Cleveland back to the top.

team the Ravens, and Cleveland got a "new" Browns team in 1999.

➔ Oops! In a 2002 game, Cleveland led the Chiefs. With zero seconds on the clock, Cleveland's Dwayne Rudd threw his helmet in joy. That was a penalty, and it gave the Chiefs a chance to try a field goal, which they made to win 40–39.

You Can Look It Up! CLEVELAND'S OFFICIAL WEBSITE: www.clevelandbrowns.com

PITTSBURGH STEELERS

One of the most successful NFL teams ever—their six Super Bowl titles are the most of all time—the Steelers started with a long dry spell. They didn't make the playoffs until 1972! They've done pretty well since then, though!

GAME 1?
1933

After winning money at a horse race, Art Rooney used the cash to buy a new NFL team. The Steelers had a slow start and went without a winning season until 1942!

 ## MAGIC MOMENT
What a Catch!

In 1972, Franco Harris caught a deflected pass—the "Immaculate Reception"—giving the Steelers their first-ever playoff win.

 ## LOWEST LOW
Worst Season

The Steelers have had some *baaad* seasons, but their 1–13 record in 1969 was their worst ever. Still, they were in the playoffs by 1972!

STUFF

HOME:
Heinz Field

SUPER BOWL TITLES: **6**

ONLY IN PITTSBURGH:
Inspired by an idea from radio man Myron Cope, Steelers fans wave yellow "Terrible Towels" during games.

STAR SEASONS!

1975 After 42 long years, owner Art Rooney finally lifted a championship trophy when the Steelers won their first Super Bowl.

1992 Running back Barry Foster set a Steelers record by rumbling for 1,690 yards.

2005 Led by QB "Big Ben" Roethlisberger, the Steelers lost only one game on the way to their fifth Super Bowl title.

The Ultimate Steeler
TERRY BRADSHAW

You get to be the *ultimate* Steeler for leading your team to four Super Bowl wins . . . and losing most of your teeth in the process. With a strong arm and famed toughness, Bradshaw guided the Steelers to four titles in six years and won two Super Bowl MVPs–as well as a place in the Hall of Fame.

#1

FUNKY FACTS

➔ What was the Pittsburgh NFL team first called? The Pirates, like the baseball team. They became the Steelers in 1940.

➔ Wanna know a secret? The name of the shape of those three things on the Steelers helmet is "hypocycloid." The colors– orange, blue, and yellow– stand for coal, iron, and fire, which are needed to make steel!

➔ So many Steelers were drafted to fight in World War II that the team was forced to combine with the Eagles in 1943 (the "Steagles") and the Cardinals in 1944 ("Card-Pitt"). Fans called the

SUPERSTAR!
TROY POLAMALU

With his long hair flowing from the back of his helmet, Pro Bowl safety Troy Polamalu races from sideline to sideline to deliver bone-jarring tackles. He's a key leader of the Steelers' mighty defense.

1944 team the "Carpets" because everyone walked all over them!

➔ In the 1990s, multitalented Kordell Stewart was known as "Slash." He played QB/WR/RB/PR. Get it?

You Can Look It Up! PITTSBURGH'S OFFICIAL WEBSITE: www.pittsburghsteelers.com

SECOND QUARTER

Well, the game's under way . . . time to check the record book. In this chapter, let's relive some of the biggest plays in NFL history. Long runs, amazing catches, game-winning scores, and more. The Catch! The Music City Miracle! The Immaculate Reception! The Twinkle-Toes Touchdown! The Drive! (Okay, one of those is fake . . . but you'll have to read the chapter to find out which one!)

INSIDE:

Steve Smith of Carolina shows how to strrrrretch for a catch!

LOOOOONG PLAYS!

Few things are more exciting in the NFL than a long touchdown play. Let's take a look at the longest ever!

109 YARDS

A record that can't be broken! No one can score a 110-yard touchdown, since they'd have to start off the field! The only 109-yard score ever came in 2007, when San Diego's Antonio Cromartie returned a missed field goal—yes, that play is legal!—the length of the field . . . and then some.

108 YARDS

In 2006, Nathan Vasher of the Bears snagged a missed field goal eight yards into the end zone and carried it all the way back for a TD. Devin Hester did the same thing in 2005, also for the Bears. And Ellis Hobbs returned a kickoff 108 yards for the Patriots in 2007.

107 YARDS

In 2002, Chris McAllister of Baltimore went this far with yet another missed field goal. In 2008, McAllister's teammate Ed Reed set the record for the longest interception return at 107 yards.

106 YARDS

Ed Reed's 107-yard interception return in 2008 broke by one yard the previous NFL record for the longest return set by . . . Ed Reed (in 2004).

LONGEST RUN EVER

On a play from scrimmage, the record can only be 99 yards. You can't take a handoff and go 100 yards . . . remember, you have to start on the 1-yard line! The only player to run 99 yards for a touchdown was Tony Dorsett of the Cowboys. He burst through the line and sprinted past the Vikings in a January 1983 Monday Night Football game.

MORE LONG STUFF

Longest Punt
Steve O'Neal whanged a punt that flew, bounced, and rolled 98 yards! He did it in 1969 for the New York Jets.

Longest Field Goals
Tom Dempsey of the Saints kicked a 63-yard field goal to win a game in 1970. Jason Elam of Denver tied that mark with a kick in 1998.

PASSING THE FIELD

Long pass plays are more common, but still, only 11 have "gone the distance"—that is, covered a defense-crushing 99 yards.

RECEIVER	PASSER	TEAM	YEAR
Bernard Berrian	Gus Frerotte	MINNESOTA	2008
Andre Davis	Jeff Garcia	CLEVELAND	2004
Marc Boerigter	Trent Green	KANSAS CITY	2002
Robert Brooks	Brett Favre	GREEN BAY	1995
Tony Martin	Stan Humphries	SAN DIEGO	1994
Mike Quick	Ron Jaworski	PHILADELPHIA	1985
Cliff Branch	Jim Plunkett	L.A. RAIDERS	1983
Gerry Allen	Sonny Jurgensen	WASHINGTON	1968
Pat Studstill	Karl Sweetan	DETROIT	1966
Bobby Mitchell	George Izo	WASHINGTON	1963
Andy Farkas	Frank Filchock	WASHINGTON	1939

RUSHING

Running plays are the basic building block of an offense. Every team needs a good running game to succeed. Let's take the handoff from the QB and run for glory with these running-back heroes.

First 1,000-yard runner

1,000 yards is considered the single-season benchmark for great runners. Reach four digits; earn a spot among the top runners. With 1,004 yards in 1934, Chicago rookie **Beattie Feathers** was the first to go beyond 999 (barely!).

The Big 2,000

If you think 1,000 is good . . . how about 2,000?! That total has been reached by only five players, including the all-time single-season record holder.

ERIC DICKERSON,* L.A. Rams
1984, 2,105 yards

JAMAL LEWIS, Baltimore
2003, 2,066 yards

◀◀ **BARRY SANDERS,** Detroit
1997, 2,053 yards

TERRELL DAVIS, Denver
1998, 2,008 yards

O.J. SIMPSON, Buffalo
1973, 2,003 yards

*Bonus: Dickerson also holds the rookie season record: 1,808 yards in 1983.

ATTACK!

One Game . . . One Runner

How far could you run in 60 minutes? Okay, how far could you run in 60 minutes with 11 enormous dudes whacking you every time you touched the ball? We thought so. Here are the best single-game rushing totals in NFL history.

MOST YARDS GAINED, SINGLE-GAME

296 Adrian Peterson▶▶
Minnesota, 2007

295 Jamal Lewis
Baltimore, 2003

278 Corey Dillon
Cincinnati, 2000

275 Walter Payton
Chicago, 1977

ULTIMATE RUNS

Our picks for the best rushing plays in NFL history:

➤ **Alan Ameche**'s one-yard plunge to win the 1958 NFL Championship Game.

➤ **Bart Starr**'s sneak to win "The Ice Bowl," the subzero 1967 NFL Championship Game.

➤ On national TV in 1978, the Oilers' **Earl Campbell** stunned the Dolphins with a legendary, game-clinching 81-yard TD run.

PASS...

If Tom Brady or Tony Romo had been around in 1905, they wouldn't have had jobs. Passing was not allowed until 1906! Now quarterbacks light up NFL scoreboards with an amazing array of bombs, outs, ins, posts, and fades. Here are some of the greatest passing records ever.

MOST CAREER PASSING YARDS:
65,127

MOST CAREER PASS ATTEMPTS:
5,720

MOST CAREER COMPLETIONS:
9,280

MOST TD PASSES:
464

◄◄One player owns ALL of those marks! The great **BRETT FAVRE** put Miami's Dan Marino in second place, reaching the No. 1 career spot in most of these categories in 2007, his final year with Green Bay. Favre played the 2008 season with the Jets.

MOST TD PASSES IN A SEASON: 50

New England's **TOM BRADY** reached that magic mark in 2007, topping Peyton Manning's 49 in 2004. Only four players have ever reached 40 TD passes in a season (Dan Marino did it twice).

MOST TD PASSES IN A GAME: 7

Five players have reached this total. **JOE KAPP** of the Vikings was the most recent, hitting the lucky number in a 1969 game.

MOST CONSECUTIVE GAMES WITH A TD PASS: 47

This record seems unbreakable! **JOHNNY UNITAS** of the Colts did it from 1956–1960. No one has come within ten games of that streak.

AND CATCH

Of course, all those passes would have been intercepted if not for the receivers who caught them. Let's meet some of the all-time greatest "hands." (The best passers from yesterday and today are profiled on pages 104-107.)

Don Hutson, Packers
First great wide receiver . . . led NFL in receiving—a record eight times . . . in 1942, had more than twice as many catches as any other player . . . 99 career TDs was the league record for 44 years!

Lance Alworth, Chargers
Known as Bambi for his leaping ability . . . combined speed and quickness like no player before him . . . helped make the long pass a big part of the AFL's popularity.

Steve Largent, Seahawks
Perhaps the best hands of all time . . . not big, but always found a way to get open . . . was the career leader in most receiving categories when he retired in 1989.

Jerry Rice, 49ers*
Perhaps the greatest overall player of all time . . . holds every receiving record worth holding . . . all-time leader in touchdowns, too.

Cris Carter, Vikings**
Caught 122 passes in a season—twice! . . . among the all-time leaders in catches, touchdowns, and receiving yards . . . had an amazing knack for making the big play.

*Also played for Raiders and Seahawks.   **Also played for Eagles and Dolphins.

THE CATCH

Of all the passes caught in all the years of the NFL, only one is known as "The Catch." San Francisco's **DWIGHT CLARK** made it to win the 1981 NFC Championship Game. QB Joe Montana threw it after backpedaling away from Dallas defenders. Clark leaped at the back of the end zone and snagged the ball with his fingertips. The play kickstarted the 49ers' 1980s dynasty . . . and got its own nickname.

TOUCHDOWN HEROES

The point of football is to outscore the other team, right? Well, that means the guys who score the most touchdowns are the biggest heroes. Some of the greatest scorers in NFL history have played recently (or are playing now, like **LaDAINIAN TOMLINSON**). Here's a list of the top ten TD machines in NFL history.

PLAYER	TOTAL TOUCHDOWNS
Jerry **Rice**	208
Emmitt **Smith**	175
Marcus **Allen**	145
Terrell **Owens***	141
LaDainian **Tomlinson***	141
Marshall **Faulk**	136
Randy **Moss***	136
Cris **Carter**	131
Marvin **Harrison***	128
Jim **Brown**	126

*Active through 2008.

THEY PUT THE "FOOT" IN FOOTBALL

Consider this page the "extra point" in a chapter dedicated to record-setting heroes. Kickers don't get much attention—except when they do something wrong! It's an odd job, actually. After three hours of giant guys smacking each other around, a little guy runs out and kicks the ball—and the giant guys win or lose. Here are the ten best field-goal kickers ever.

Most Career Field Goals Made

PLAYER	FGS
Morten Andersen	565
Gary Anderson	538
Matt Stover*	462
John Carney*	460
Jason Elam*	424
Jason Hanson*	406
John Kasay*	386
Nick Lowery	383
Jan Stenerud	373
Norm Johnson	366

MOST ACCURATE

These guys made the highest percentage of their field-goal attempts; all of them made at least 100 field goals.

PLAYER	PCT.
Nick Folk*	86.79
Mike Vanderjagt	86.47
Nate Kaeding*	86.13
Robbie Gould*	85.94
Shayne Graham*	85.64

*Active through 2008.

GREAT MOMENTS

Some NFL events are so amazing, so momentous, so incredible . . . that they get their own names! Every NFL fan worth his foam No. 1 finger and replica team jersey knows what these names mean. And yes, Giants and Steelers fans, we'll cover great Super Bowl moments in a later chapter—don't worry.

IMMACULATE RECEPTION

Late in a 1972 playoff game, the Steelers trailed the Raiders. Pittsburgh's Terry Bradshaw fired a pass downfield. It bounced off one (or two?) players and was about to hit the ground when Franco Harris of the Steelers nabbed it. He rumbled for a game-winning score! Did the pass hit a Steeler? At the time, that would have been illegal. The NFL later changed the rule so the ball can ricochet off anyone.

THE DRIVE

Down by a TD against Cleveland with 98 yards to cover in just over five minutes. For John Elway—no problem. The Broncos' great QB led his team on a 15-play march that ended in a game-tying score. Denver won the 1986 AFC title game in overtime and headed to the Super Bowl.

THE COMEBACK

In a 1992 playoff game, Buffalo trailed the Oilers 35–3 in the third quarter. Many Bills fans left for home—bad move. The Bills roared back, scoring four touchdowns in less than seven minutes. Buffalo tied Houston and forced overtime—and then won on a field goal. The 32-point comeback is still the biggest in NFL history.

MUSIC CITY MIRACLE

In the state that country music and Elvis Presley made famous, the Tennessee Titans dreamed up one of the NFL's most famous plays. During a 1999 playoff game, Buffalo took the lead with just 16 seconds left. Tennessee then received the kickoff. Lorenzo Neal caught the ball and handed it to Frank Wycheck, who threw a cross-field lateral to Kevin Dyson. Dyson romped past the stunned Bills for a 75-yard, game-winning, miraculous score.

HOUSTON
TEXANS

One of the NFL's newest teams, the Texans are still establishing their identity. They've had a few bright moments, but they're not yet among the league's top teams. Sharing the Lone Star State with the Cowboys doesn't help!

GAME 1?
2002

Houston was without an NFL team after the Oilers (who are now the Tennessee Titans) left in 1997. Five years later, the Texans burst onto the scene with a 19–10 upset of Dallas.

 MAGIC MOMENT
Before the Games

Perhaps the biggest day in Texans history was the day the NFL announced Houston would get a new team, beating out other cities.

 LOWEST LOW
Really Bad

The Texans got better every year until 2005, when they hit a huge roadblock, winning only two games. Back to the drawing board!

STUFF

HOME:
Reliant Stadium

SUPER BOWL TITLES: 0

ONLY IN HOUSTON:
Along with a livestock show (see Funky Facts), fans can watch monster trucks, pro wrestling, and Elmo at Reliant.

STAR SEASONS!

2004
David Carr set a pretty high standard for future Texans QBs when he set a team record with 3,531 passing yards.

2008
Rookie running back Steve Slaton was not expected to start. But he set a team record with 1,282 rushing yards.

2008
Andre Johnson set team records for receptions, receiving yards, and touchdown catches.

The Ultimate Texan

DAVID CARR

This award goes to Carr based partly on history (he was the first QB in Texans history) and partly out of pity (he was sacked a record 76 times in 2002). Plus, he helped the team win the first game it ever played! Carr did the best he could with a tough job, though he has since moved on to backup roles with other teams.

FUNKY FACTS

➜ The Texans' new home, Reliant Stadium, was built with help from a livestock and rodeo show that also uses the massive place.

➜ Good start! Most expansion teams start off with pretty terrible seasons. The Texans were no different. However, they did win their first home game, beating the Dallas Cowboys 19–10.

➜ In 2009, the Houston Texans became the last NFL team to make its first appearance in a Monday Night Football game. They're also (so far) the only NFL team without a division title.

SUPERSTAR!

ANDRE JOHNSON

Opposing defenses do all they can to stop him, but Johnson still gets open. He busted out in 2008, catching 115 passes and scoring eight touchdowns.

➜ The Texans have a winning record against only one of their AFC South opponents. They are 8–6 (through 2008) against the Jacksonville Jaguars.

You Can Look It Up! HOUSTON'S OFFICIAL WEBSITE: www.houstontexans.com

INDIANAPOLIS COLTS

In the past decade, the Colts have become one of the NFL's elite teams. It's not the first time they've risen to the top, however. Both in Baltimore and Indy, fans have had many reasons to ride these Colts into the sunset.

GAME 1? 1953

There was another Colts team that lasted only one season in the NFL (1950). The current Colts started in 1953 in Baltimore. In 1984, they moved to Indianapolis. (See Funky Facts.)

MAGIC MOMENT
Greatest Game Ever

Johnny Unitas led the Colts to a dramatic overtime victory over the Giants in the 1958 NFL Championship Game.

LOWEST LOW
Hobbled Colts

After doing pretty well in the 1980s, the Colts hit the skids. In 1991, they won only one game, their worst season ever.

STUFF

HOME:
Lucas Oil Stadium

SUPER BOWL TITLES: 2

ONLY IN INDIANAPOLIS:
The Colts' home stadium features a "moving window" at one end. It can open to reveal the downtown skyline.

STAR SEASONS!

2000 Edgerrin James rushed for 1,709 yards, leading the league for the second straight year.

2002 Receiver Marvin Harrison set an NFL record by catching an amazing 143 passes!

2004 Peyton Manning set a new NFL record by throwing 49 touchdown passes. Tom Brady later topped him with 50, though.

The Ultimate Colt
JOHNNY UNITAS

Some experts put "Johnny U." at the top of the list of all-time best QBs. Unitas once threw a touchdown pass in 47 straight games. He was also tough, playing through many injuries. Plus, he called all of the team's plays, something even Peyton Manning doesn't do today. Unitas remains "Mr. Colt."

FUNKY FACTS

→ The Colts won their first Super Bowl in dramatic fashion. In Super Bowl V, rookie Jim O'Brien kicked a game-winning field goal with just five seconds left!

→ The Baltimore Colts had a volunteer marching band that performed before games and at halftime. Most were not full-time musicians—just fans who loved to play!

→ When the Colts won Super Bowl XLI, Tony Dungy became the first African American head coach of a Super Bowl winner. He later became the author of three best-selling books!

→ The Colts moved to Indy in 1984. One problem: They didn't

SUPERSTAR!
PEYTON MANNING

Who else? Manning is "the man" in Indy, where he has made every start since entering the league in 1998. He has set dozens of team records and has also become famous for his funny TV commercials.

tell anyone they were moving. Trucks came in the dark of night to "steal" the team from Baltimore. Fans there never forgave Colts team owner Robert Irsay for his sneakiness.

You Can Look It Up! INDIANAPOLIS'S OFFICIAL WEBSITE: www.colts.com

JACKSONVILLE JAGUARS

Few expansion teams have gotten as good as quickly as the Jaguars did. Led by lefty QB Mark Brunell, the Jags nearly made the Super Bowl in their second season! They've had their ups and downs since then.

GAME 1?
1995

The Jaguars joined the NFL as an expansion team. Their home city of Jacksonville is one of the smallest cities to field an NFL team. Green Bay's still smaller, though!

 ## MAGIC MOMENT
1996 AFC Playoffs

First the Jags stunned the Bills 30–27. Then they dethroned top-ranked Denver, also 30–27. A loss to the Patriots ended their dream.

 ## LOWEST LOW
Slow Start

The Jags played their first season like they were new to football, not just the NFL. They won four games but didn't play well.

STUFF

HOME:
Jacksonville Municipal Stadium

SUPER BOWL TITLES: 0

ONLY IN JAX:
A Jacksonville sports-writer proposed to his girlfriend via the score-board at a 2008 Jags game. She said "Yes!"

STAR SEASONS!

1996 Mark Brunell set a team record by passing for 4,367 yards as the Jags shocked everyone.

1999 With a regular-season record of 14–2, the Jaguars posted the best mark in the NFL. In their first playoff game, they whomped Miami 62–7! Unfortunately, they were upset the next week by the Titans.

2003 Fred Taylor ran for 1,572 yards, setting a team record.

The Ultimate Jaguar
FRED TAYLOR

Taylor is one of those players who just does his job, year in and year out. This ex-Jag has never gotten the headlines, but he gets the job done. The Jaguars' all-time leader in games played, he has topped 11,000 rushing yards for his career, a total that places him among the top 20 runners all-time.

FUNKY FACTS

➔ A little help: The Jaguars got a chance to make their amazing 1996 playoff run by beating Atlanta on the last day of the season. (They won only because Falcons star kicker Morten Andersen missed an easy field goal.)

➔ Can't win for winning: A big fourth-down run by QB David Garrard in a 2007 playoff game set up the game-winning field goal. The win was tainted when officials later said they missed a holding penalty.

➔ Weird Injury Department: For some reason, coach Jack Del Rio put a stump and an ax in the locker room in 2003.

SUPERSTAR!
MAURICE JONES-DREW

The man they call "Mo-Jo" is a bowling ball of a runner and just about as hard to stop as one. Skilled at both running and catching passes, he has scored 40 touchdowns during his first three NFL seasons.

Punter Chris Hanson tried to chop the stump, gashed his foot with the ax, and missed the rest of the season.

You Can Look It Up! JACKSONVILLE'S OFFICIAL WEBSITE: www.jaguars.com

TENNESSEE
TITANS

The Titans take their name from some Greek gods. And on occasion, they have definitely played like gods. In the land of Elvis, the Titans have given their fans thrills and miracles, while leaving folks back in Houston with the new guys.

GAME 1?
1960

The Titans began in 1960 as the Houston Oilers of the AFL. The AFL merged with the NFL in 1970. The team moved to Tennessee in 1997; they became the Titans in '99.

 ## MAGIC MOMENT
Super Bowl XXXIV

In their only Super Bowl, the Titans were driving toward the game-tying score with just seconds to go. It seemed like a miracle finish . . .

 ## LOWEST LOW
Super Bowl XXXIV

. . . until they were foiled on the last play of the game. The Titans' Kevin Dyson was tackled by the Rams' Mike Jones on the one-yard line!

STUFF

HOME:
LP Field

SUPER BOWL TITLES: 0

ONLY IN NASHVILLE:
Look for fans wearing odd hats that spout bright-orange foam "fire," taking their cue from the team logo.

STAR SEASONS!

1980 The amazing Earl Campbell ran for 1,934 yards, winning the league rushing title and setting a team record.

1991 Rifle-armed Warren Moon set a team record with 4,690 passing yards. He holds the team's top five single-season marks.

2008 The Titans knocked off the Colts, winning the AFC South for the first time since 2002.

The Ultimate Oiler/Titan

GEORGE BLANDA

Blanda played QB for several teams, including seven seasons with Houston. He helped the team win the first two AFL titles (1960, 1961). He was also a fine kicker. Blanda ended up playing until he was 48, setting (since-broken) NFL records for most games played and points scored.

FUNKY FACTS

→ While in Houston, one of the team's coaches was "Bum" Phillips, who was well known for wearing cowboy boots on the sidelines.

→ Dan Pastorini, who quarterbacked the Oilers in the 1970s, had a post-NFL career as the owner and driver of a drag racer.

→ The Titans pulled off the "Music City Miracle" to win a 1999 playoff game. Down by one point on the last play of the game, a Titan threw a cross-field lateral to a teammate, who ran 75 yards for the TD!

SUPERSTAR!
ROB BIRONAS

A kicker? Well, when you set an NFL record with eight field goals in one game, make a game-winning 60-yarder as time runs out, and win several others with last-minute boots . . . then sure, a superstar kicker!

→ The Titans once boasted a kicker, Al Del Greco, who was also probably the best golfer in the NFL.

You Can Look It Up! TENNESSEE'S OFFICIAL WEBSITE: www.tennesseetitans.com

DENVER BRONCOS

The pride of Mile High City, the Broncos were terrible for a long time—but when they were good, they were awesome! Denver lost four Super Bowls before they finally won one (in the 1997 season). Then they won the following year, too!

GAME 1? 1960

The Broncos played their first season in 1960. They were part of the new American Football League (AFL). In 1970, the AFL merged with the NFL.

 ## MAGIC MOMENT
Super Bowl XXXII

John Elway led the Broncos to their first NFL championship, defeating the Green Bay Packers 31–24 in Super Bowl XXXII.

 ## LOWEST LOW
Super Bowl XXIV

They were the best of the AFC, but the Broncos were broken by the NFC-champ 49ers in Super Bowl XXIV, losing (ouch!) 55–10!

STUFF

HOME:
INVESCO Field at Mile High

SUPER BOWL TITLES: **2**

ONLY IN DENVER:
Ten-hut! After scoring touchdowns, Broncos sometimes stand and give the Mile High Salute!

STAR SEASONS!

1998 Terrell Davis set two team records: He ran for 2,008 yards and scored 23 touchdowns. No big surprise for a guy named "TD"!

2001 Rod Smith caught 11 touchdown passes and had a team-record 113 receptions.

2004 Jake "The Snake" Plummer passed for 4,089 yards and 27 touchdowns. For a short while, Denver fans said, "Elway who?"

The Ultimate Bronco
JOHN ELWAY

The fabled quarterback holds all the team's career passing marks. After losing three Super Bowls, he led Denver to a pair of Super Bowl titles. Elway was a master at rallying his team to come-from-behind victories. Elway boasted a strong arm, the ability to escape tacklers, and some serious toughness. He's in the Hall of Fame.

FUNKY FACTS

→ Denver's early uniforms featured socks with vertical brown and yellow stripes. After the team lost too often, it burned the socks to "put that in the past." It didn't work . . . the Broncos kept losing. But they did get better-looking socks!

→ One of the team's longtime fans came to games wearing only a barrel held up by suspenders. Barrel Man was one of the NFL's most famous wacky fans!

→ Thanks to his strong leg (and maybe mile-high Denver's thin air) Jason Elam tied an NFL record in 1998 by kicking a 63-yard field goal.

SUPERSTAR!
CHAMP BAILEY

Bailey is not only one of the NFL's fastest players, he's also one of the league's best cornerbacks. He leads the Denver defense and always covers the opponent's best receiver.

→ The giant white horse atop Denver's stadium is named "Bucky." He's a bronco. Bucky... bucking ... get it?

You Can Look It Up! DENVER'S OFFICIAL WEBSITE: www.denverbroncos.com

KANSAS CITY CHIEFS

The Chiefs have had some pretty good stretches of success . . . just not recently. They haven't reached the Super Bowl for 40 years, but they have boasted some outstanding players during that time.

GAME 1?
1960

The Chiefs started out as the Dallas Texans in the first year of the American Football League (AFL). The team moved to Kansas City in 1963 and changed to its current name.

MAGIC MOMENT
Super Bowl IV

In the final game before the AFL merged with the NFL, the Chiefs beat the Vikings to earn the AFL's second Super Bowl win.

LOWEST LOW
They Hate '08

The Chiefs set a team record for losses, racking up 14 "L"s. Only the Lions' 0–16 record kept K.C. from finishing at the bottom.

STUFF

HOME:
Arrowhead Stadium

SUPER BOWL TITLES: **1**

ONLY IN KANSAS CITY:
KC Wolf, the team's mascot, once tackled a fan who ran onto the field during a game. The crowd cheered the "security wolf."

STAR SEASONS!

1990 Derrick Thomas became a rare linebacker to lead the NFL in sacks, with 20.

2003 Priest Holmes set a new NFL record by running for 27 touchdowns! His record was later topped, but what a year!

2006 Larry Johnson set a team record with 1,789 rushing yards. He also scored 19 times, thrilling fantasy football fans.

The Ultimate Chief
LEN DAWSON

Accurate and dependable, Dawson put together a Hall of Fame career, playing 14 years with the Texans and Chiefs after five seasons with other teams. He led the AFL in passer rating three times. The franchise won three AFL titles under Dawson, who holds all the team's major career passing records.

#1

FUNKY FACTS

→ The Chiefs' Hall of Fame coach Hank Stram was famous for always wearing a jacket and tie on the sidelines.

→ Kansas City's long-time owner Lamar Hunt also was a big soccer fan. He started several pro soccer teams and helped found Major League Soccer.

→ In a 1985 game, K.C. receiver Stephone Paige caught passes for a then-record 309 yards!

→ K.C. kicker Jan Stenerud is the only member of the Hall of Fame who only played kicker.

→ Chiefs running back Christian Okoye had one of the coolest

SUPERSTAR!
DWAYNE BOWE

The speedy legs and sticky hands of wide receiver Bowe have been a bright spot in the Chiefs' recent gloomy seasons. Bowe topped 1,000 yards for the first time in 2008.

nicknames. Due to his birthplace and powerful running style, fans called him the "Nigerian Nightmare"! He led the NFL in 1989 with 1,480 rushing yards.

You Can Look It Up! KANSAS CITY'S OFFICIAL WEBSITE: www.kcchiefs.com

OAKLAND
RAIDERS

Few sports teams are as loved—or hated—as the Raiders. Their fans are loyal, fierce, and intense. Their enemies are in the millions! The Raiders love to be hated and look forward to casting fear into opponents' hearts again.

GAME 1?
1960

The Raiders were part of the AFL. In 1970, the AFL merged with the NFL. From 1982–1994, the team played in Los Angeles before returning to Oakland.

 ## MAGIC MOMENT
Super Bowl XVIII

The Redskins were favored to win, but the Raiders crushed them 38–9 to earn their third Super Bowl title.

 ## LOWEST LOW
2003 onward

A proud team has fallen on tough times. Since losing the Super Bowl in the 2002 season, the Raiders' overall record is a dismal 24–72.

STUFF

HOME:
Oakland Coliseum

SUPER BOWL TITLES: **3**

ONLY IN OAKLAND:
Devoted fans dress in amazing costumes covered with skulls, silver paint, spikes, chains, and other scary gear.

STAR SEASONS!

1976 The Raiders capped off five straight play-off seasons with their first Super Bowl victory.

1985 Marcus Allen set a team record and led the NFL with 1,759 rushing yards.

2002 Veteran QB Rich Gannon led the Raiders to the Super Bowl while leading the NFL with a team-record 4,689 passing yards.

The Ultimate Raider

AL DAVIS

Not a player—he's the owner! No single person embodies an NFL team more than Davis. He took over as coach in 1963 and later led a group that bought the team. He has had the final word on everything in Raider Nation for four decades. His slogans "Just win, baby!" and "A tradition of excellence" define the Raider Way.

FUNKY FACTS

→ Raiders QB Daryle Lamonica got his nickname "The Mad Bomber" for his skill at throwing long passes, or "bombs."

→ The Raiders forced a change in NFL rules. In 1978, they won a game on the last play when Ken Stabler intentionally fumbled the ball into the end zone, where Dave Casper recovered it for the win. The NFL later made the play illegal!

→ Hall of Famer John Madden, who coached the Raiders from 1969–1978, is now, of course, much more famous for putting his name on the awesomely popular Madden NFL video games.

SUPERSTAR!

DARREN McFADDEN

At the University of Arkansas, McFadden was one of the best running backs in the country. The Raiders made him their first pick in 2008, and they're depending on him to be a superstar in the pros, too.

→ The Raiders may be known as a pretty rough-and-tumble team, but give them credit for this: the team's Amy Trask was the first woman to become the chief executive of an NFL franchise.

You Can Look It Up! OAKLAND'S OFFICIAL WEBSITE: www.raiders.com

SAN DIEGO
CHARGERS

The team's fight song includes the words, "San Diego . . . Superchargers!" Well, other than one loss in the big game, the Chargers haven't really been "super." But they have been pretty good, thanks in large part to a guy named L.T.

GAME 1?
1960

The Chargers started out in Los Angeles as one of the original AFL teams. They only played one season there before moving to San Diego in 1961. The AFL merged with the NFL in 1970.

 ## MAGIC MOMENT
AFL Champs!

The Chargers powered their way to their only championship in 1963, winning the AFL title by whomping the Boston Patriots 51–10.

 ## LOWEST LOW
Nearly 0-fer '00

It took a late 52-yard field goal to clinch a 17–16 win over K.C. for San Diego to grab its *only* win of this forgettable season.

STUFF

HOME:
Qualcomm Stadium

SUPER BOWL TITLES: **0**

ONLY IN SAN DIEGO:
The Chargers' unofficial mascot is a fan named Dan. He dresses in a lightning-gold costume and goes by the name Boltman.

STAR SEASONS!

1981 Dan Fouts set a team record with one of the best passing seasons ever, throwing for 4,802 yards.

2006 What a year! RB LaDainian Tomlinson broke the NFL record with 31 TDs in a season. He also led the NFL with 1,815 rushing yards.

2008 Philip Rivers set a team record—and led the NFL—with 34 touchdown passes.

The Ultimate Charger

LANCE ALWORTH

He hated the nickname, but to NFL fans, Alworth will always be "Bambi." The Disney deer came to mind when fans watched Alworth leap, spin, and sprint on AFL fields in the 1960s. He became the first player who spent most of his career in the AFL to make the Hall of Fame.

#1

FUNKY FACTS

→ A fan named Gerry came up with the name "Chargers" in a newspaper contest. His other ideas included Ocelots, Residents, and Balboans.

→ San Diego's John Hadl was the last quarterback to wear a number above 19. New rules mean that no other QB will ever wear his No. 21.

→ Hot and cold in 1982: First, San Diego won a playoff game in overtime, and Kellen Winslow played so hard he sweated off 13 pounds! Then, a week later, they lost the AFC Championship Game to Cincinnati while playing in a mind-numbing −59 degrees wind chill!

SUPERSTAR!

LaDAINIAN TOMLINSON

The Chargers boast the NFL's most famous running back. In only eight seasons, "LT" has climbed to fourth place all-time in touchdowns. He set the single-season record with 31 in 2006.

→ The Chargers came up on the short end of a weird game in 2008. They lost to the Steelers in a game that finished with the only 11–10 final score in NFL history.

You Can Look It Up! SAN DIEGO'S OFFICIAL WEBSITE: www.chargers.com

THIRD QUARTER

Time to focus on the D. The tacklers, the sackers, the ball-hawkers. The rough-and-tumble "bringers of the pain train," as one player memorably said. The old saying in the NFL is "defense wins championships." And if you put all the guys featured in this chapter on one team, you'd win an awful lot of championships! We've got some non-defense stuff in here, too, to lighten the mood a little.

INSIDE:

Dogpile on Maroney! Dogpile on Maroney!

SACK MASTERS

If you're a quarterback, you might want to turn the page. This spread could hurt! Because here we celebrate the guys who hunt QBs. They sack the quarterback, which means they tackle him behind the line of scrimmage before he can pass. The term "sack" was invented in the late 1960s by Hall-of-Fame defensive end Deacon Jones. The NFL didn't keep official stats for sacks until 1982. Here are the best sack artists since then.

ONE-GAME SACK MASTERS

You'd think after a guy makes four or five sacks, the other team might try to block him. The opponents of these single-game sack champs apparently didn't get that message. In a 1990 game vs. Seattle, the Chiefs' Derrick Thomas nabbed an all-time record seven sacks. Thomas also had six sacks in a 1998 game vs. the Raiders. Two other players have also made six sacks in one game: Fred Dean of the 49ers (vs. New Orleans in 1983), and Osi Umenyiora of the Giants (vs. Philadelphia in 2007).

Career Sack Leaders

SACKS	PLAYER (YEARS)
200	**Bruce Smith** (1985–2003)
198	**Reggie White** (1985–1998, 2000)
160	**Kevin Greene** (1985–1999)
150.5*	**Chris Doleman** (1985–1999)
141.5	**Michael Strahan** (1993–2007)
137.5	**John Randle** (1990–2003)
137.5	**Richard Dent** (1983–1997)

(*.5? How can you get half a sack? If two players converge to whomp the QB at the same time, each gets credit for half of the sack.)

Single-Season Sack Leaders

SACKS	PLAYER, TEAM	YEAR
22.5	**Michael Strahan,** Giants	2001
22.0	**Mark Gastineau,** Jets	1984
21.0	**Chris Doleman,** Vikings	1989
21.0	**Reggie White,** Eagles	1987
20.5	**Lawrence Taylor,** Giants	1986
20.0	**DeMarcus Ware,** Cowboys	2008
20.0	**Derrick Thomas,** Chiefs	1990

The Other Side of the Sack

What about all the poor quarterbacks who were on the other end of these sacks? Who felt the pain most often? Great as he was, John Elway was sacked more often than any other passer: 516 times! David Carr of the Houston Texans holds the painful single-season record with 76 in 2002. Both guys look forward to seeing their names leave that part of the record book!

THE THIEVES

When a pass is thrown, it's anybody's ball. The offense, of course, has an advantage. They know where the ball is supposed to go. But the defense has every right to pick it off, and when they do—interception!

Top Ten Interception Leaders of All-Time

Paul **Krause**	81
Emlen **Tunnell**	79
Rod **Woodson**	71
Night Train **Lane**	68
Ken **Riley**	65
‹‹‹Ronnie **Lott**	63
Dick **LeBeau**	62
Dave **Brown**	62
Emmitt **Thomas**	58
Johnny **Robinson**	57
Eugene **Robinson**	57
Bobby **Boyd**	57
Mel **Blount**	57
Everson **Walls**	57

Who's Next?

Darren Sharper (54) and Ty Law (52) are the two active players with the best chance to join these all-time greats.

MOST INTERCEPTION RETURN TOUCHDOWNS

12 Rod Woodson
9 Aeneas Williams
9 Deion Sanders
9 Ken Houston
8 Darren Sharper*
8 Eric Allen

The Other Side of the Interception

Of course, these players would have nothing to catch if it weren't for inaccurate passers. Here's a nod to the guys who threw all these picks.

MOST INTERCEPTIONS, CAREER
BRETT FAVRE,* 310

Favre's record is probably safe. The active player with the second-most interceptions is Kerry Collins, who has thrown 179 passes to the other team.

MOST INTERCEPTIONS, SINGLE-SEASON
GEORGE BLANDA, 42
for the Houston Oilers in the AFL in 1962

Blanda is also safe. No passer has topped even 30 picks in a season since Vinny Testaverde threw 35 picks with the Buccaneers in 1988.

MOST PICKS, SEASON

14	Night Train Lane ▲ Rams, 1952
13	Lester Hayes Raiders, 1980
13	Spec Sanders N.Y. Yanks, 1950
13	Dan Sandifer Redskins, 1948

*Active through 2008.

HARD GUYS

Playing in the NFL is tough. It's hard. It hurts. It's dangerous, in fact. Players wear pads and they train carefully, but sometimes they get hurt. Some of these injuries are serious enough to sideline players—or even end their careers.

Injuries are no joke. And we definitely do not recommend playing through them. That's a good way to get sidelined for good. But here are some (ouch!) stories of (ow!) players who, for better or worse (oof!), played through (dang, that hurts!) pain or other physical ailments.

Rocky Bleier

Getting tackled is one thing; getting hit by shrapnel is another. Bleier earned medals for his military service in Vietnam, where he was wounded by a grenade blast. The former college star recovered to help the Steelers win four Super Bowls.

Tom Dempsey

Born without half a right foot and with only half a right arm, he played offensive line in college. In the pros, he was a standout kicker who booted field goals—with that half-foot!

Dick "Night Train" Lane

He had what he called an upset stomach before a 1962 playoff game. He played anyway. Two days later, he had to have his appendix removed!

> "If you come out of a game without bruises, you should be in a different job."
> —CARDINALS SAFETY LARRY WILSON

Johnny Unitas

One of football's toughest quarterbacks, he once had his nose broken in a game. He packed his bleeding nostrils with gauze and put his helmet back on. He missed one play.

Larry Wilson

The Cardinals safety played in a 1965 game with casts on both hands. He still intercepted a pass, though! His 34-yard return set up a key touchdown.

Jack Youngblood

Youngblood broke his left leg—and kept playing! He finished the 1979 NFC Championship Game and then played Super Bowl XIV wearing a leg brace!

MANY HAPPY RETURNS

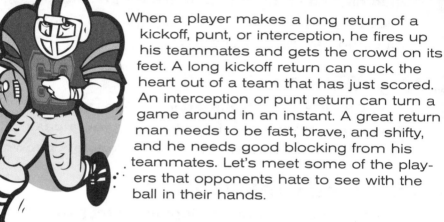

When a player makes a long return of a kickoff, punt, or interception, he fires up his teammates and gets the crowd on its feet. A long kickoff return can suck the heart out of a team that has just scored. An interception or punt return can turn a game around in an instant. A great return man needs to be fast, brave, and shifty, and he needs good blocking from his teammates. Let's meet some of the players that opponents hate to see with the ball in their hands.

MOST KICKOFF-RETURN TOUCHDOWNS

CAREER

Five players have returned six kickoffs for touchdowns:
Ollie Matson, Gale Sayers, Travis Williams, Mel Gray, Dante Hall

SINGLE-SEASON

Only two players have returned four kickoffs for TDs in one season: **Travis Williams** (Packers) in 1967 and **Cecil Turner** (Bears) in 1970.

MOST PUNT-RETURN TOUCHDOWNS (CAREER)

10	**Eric Metcalf**
9	**Brian Mitchell**
8	**Rick Upchurch**
8	**Desmond Howard**
8	**Jack Christiansen**

The Amazing DEVIN HESTER

In 2006, a speedy rookie return man busted into the NFL. Devin Hester of the Chicago Bears stunned the league by returning five kicks (three punts and two kickoffs) for touchdowns. The next year, he topped himself, tying the NFL's season record with four punt-return TDs, while adding two more kickoff-return scores. That's 11 touchdown returns in two years—the greatest two-season stretch ever!

Most Kickoff-Return Yards

Brian Mitchell returned kickoffs for nearly eight miles (14,014 yards) in his 14-year NFL career. **MarTay Jenkins** holds the single-season record with 2,186 yards in 2000. He had help, of course—his Arizona team was a bad one that gave up a lot of points . . . meaning more kickoffs for Jenkins to return!

THE WEDGE

On most successful kickoff returns, there is a pair of players who don't get enough credit. They just get all the bruises. They are "the wedge." These two players are assigned to come together as the kick returner catches the ball. They line up and wait to block the first "wedge-buster" rolling down the field toward them. If they can be more like a wall than a group of bowling pins, the return man has a shot at breaking a long run.

TALKIN'
FOOTBALL

Football has a language all its own. You probably already know about *blitz*, *sack*, *pickoff*, and *touchdown*. But what about the really cool, insider stuff? Well, here at the **Scholastic Ultimate Guide**, we can help. Learn these words, and you'll be able to talk the talk at any football game.

THE ROCK = the football
THE HOUSE = the end zone
As in, "Carry the rock to the house."

CHAIN CREW
The people who carry the sideline markers, including the ten-yard first-down chain.

CLOTHESLINE
An illegal tackle made by whacking a guy across the facemask with your forearm. Don't try this at home!

GUNNER
One of two players on the far outside of a punting team's formation. They are the only players who can race ahead of the punt to try to tackle the punt returner.

HAIL MARY
A high, long pass, late in a half or a game, that is thrown up like a prayer . . . in hope that it will be answered with a touchdown!

PANCAKE
A very hard block that knocks the opposing player to the ground, flat as a . . . pancake. Can also be a verb: "He really pancaked that linebacker."

POOCH KICK
No, not a punt by a dog! This is a high, short punt designed to be downed near the opponent's goal line.

RED ZONE
The 20 yards before the defense's goal line.

SNOT-BUBBLER

A tackle that is so hard that the tacklee has . . . well, you get the picture. A synonym would be "slobber-knocker."

THE SWIM

No, it's not how players cool off after a game . . . this is a move that a defensive lineman uses to get past a blocker. He wheels his arms like he's swimming, trying to knock the blocker aside.

THE TRENCHES

The part of the line of scrimmage from tackle to tackle, where the offensive and defensive lines crash together each play.

WILL, MIKE, AND SAM

Names given to the weak-side, middle, and strong-side linebackers. (Just in case you don't know, the offense's strong side is the side where the tight end lines up; the weak side is the other side of the formation.)

ALLIGATOR ARMS

When a receiver is worried he'll get snot-bubbled (see above), and doesn't stretch his arms out to make a catch–he has these.

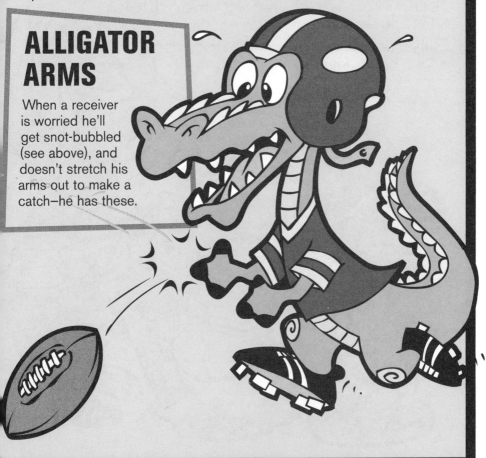

THE STORK, THE

GREAT FOOTBALL NICKNAME

Football is a colorful sport with bright uniforms and big personalities. Though today's teams and players don't have as many great nicknames as they did in the past, you can still find some fun ways to describe teams, players, or groups Here's a rundown of our all-time favorite NFL nicknames.

Players

Lou **"The Toe"** Groza

✖ Not from a gross digit . . . he was a kicker.

Ted **"The Mad Stork"** Hendricks

✖ Tall and lean and mean.

Billy **"White Shoes"** Johnson

✖ Take one guess.

OE, & THE HOGS

Dick "Night Train" Lane
✖ Named for a famous song.

"Broadway" Joe Namath
✖ After a glitzy New York City street.

"Neon" Deion "Prime Time" Sanders
✖ Two nicknames for a colorful guy.

Ken "The Snake" Stabler
✖ A gambler and a rambler.

Randy "The Manster" White
✖ Half man, half monster.

Elbert "Ickey" Woods
✖ Anything's better than Elbert!

Teams and Groups

Air Coryell
✖ Pass-oriented Chargers of the 1980s; named for coach Don.

Fearsome Foursome
✖ L.A. Rams' mighty defensive front four in the 1960s.

Greatest Show on Turf
✖ High-scoring Rams offense of the late 1990s.

The Hogs
✖ Redskins' 1980s offensive line.

Monsters of the Midway
✖ Longtime nickname for Da Bears.

Orange Crush
✖ Denver's 1970s defense.

Purple People Eaters
✖ Minnesota's 1970s defense.

Steel Curtain
✖ Pittsburgh's defense of the 1970s.

New York Sack Exchange
✖ Jets' defensive line of the early '80s.

DAWG POUND

While some groups of NFL fans get nicknames, none are more famous than the end-zone dwellers in Cleveland. Fans in "The Dawg Pound" wear rubber dog masks and used to throw dog biscuits at opposing players.

DALLAS
COWBOYS

Their rivals may grumble at the nickname "America's Team," but the Cowboys do boast fans from all over the country. When you've won as often as they have, making friends and attracting fans is pretty easy!

GAME 1?
1960

The Cowboys joined the NFL in 1960 as an expansion team. They didn't start out too well, going 0–11–1 in their first season. In fact, they didn't have a winning season until 1966!

 ## MAGIC MOMENT
Super Bowl XXX

The Cowboys capped one of the best dynasties ever with their third Super Bowl title in four seasons, beating Pittsburgh 27–17.

 ## LOWEST LOW
Bright Future?

Despite a roster filled with players who would end up as Hall of Famers, the Cowboys still finished with a 1–15 record in 1989.

STUFF

HOME:
Cowboys Stadium*

SUPER BOWL TITLES: **5**

ONLY IN DALLAS:
A hole in the Cowboys' old stadium roof was said to be there "so God can watch his favorite team."

*New name still to be chosen.

STAR SEASONS!

1977 First-round draft pick Tony Dorsett ran for more than 1,000 yards (1,007) as a rookie, and the Cowboys won the Super Bowl.

1995 Emmitt Smith's team-record 1,773 rushing yards were part of what would end up as an NFL career record of 18,355 yards.

2007 Tony Romo set a pair of impressive team records: 36 TD passes and 4,211 passing yards.

The Ultimate Cowboy
ROGER STAUBACH

Known as "Roger the Dodger" for his scrambling ability, Staubach led the Cowboys to four Super Bowls, winning two. He spent five years in the U.S. Navy after winning the Heisman Trophy in 1963. After he joined Dallas, they never had a losing season with him as QB. Staubach was an easy pick for the Hall of Fame.

FUNKY FACTS

→ The Cowboys franchise was first called the Steers, then the Rangers. Before they played any games, however, they settled on Cowboys. Whew!

→ What a run! From 1966 to 1985, the Cowboys had a winning record each season for an NFL-record 20 straight years.

→ Hall of Fame defensive tackle Bob Lilly is known as "Mr. Cowboy" for his long record of success with the team.

→ The Cowboys' amazing new home stadium, which opened in 2009, will be the site of Super Bowl XLV.

SUPERSTAR!
TONY ROMO

Romo burst onto the scene in 2007, setting team records for passing yards, TDs, and completions. Though slowed by a broken finger in 2008, he's expected to come back strong.

→ In Super Bowl V, Chuck Howley of the Cowboys became the only player from a losing team to win the game's MVP award.

You Can Look It Up! DALLAS'S OFFICIAL WEBSITE: www.dallascowboys.com

NEW YORK
GIANTS

One of the NFL's oldest teams, the Giants have often been among the very best. They won their first NFL title in 1927 and their most recent in 2007. In between, they've featured some of the greatest players in football history.

GAME 1?
1925

Tim Mara paid the NFL $500 to start a team in America's biggest city. He "borrowed" the Giants name from a pro baseball team that also played in New York City at the time.

 ## MAGIC MOMENT
Super Bowl XXI

Though they'd won championships in the past, the Giants didn't earn their first Super Bowl title until 1986, beating Denver 39–20.

 ## LOWEST LOW
A Comedown

Only three years after playing in the NFL title game, the Giants won just one game in 1966, the worst season in their long history.

STUFF

HOME:
Giants Stadium

SUPER BOWL TITLES: **3**

ONLY IN NEW JERSEY:
The Giants and Jets are the only NFL teams to share a stadium. And they'll both move to the same new stadium in 2010.

STAR SEASONS!

1963 QB Y.A. Tittle set a then-league record by tossing 36 touchdown passes.

1986 Pass-rushing linebacker Lawrence "L.T." Taylor led the NFL with 20.5 sacks, as the Giants roared to their first Super Bowl win.

2005 Running back Tiki Barber set a team record by rambling for 1,860 yards. Tiki is the club's leading career rusher, too.

The Ultimate Giant
STEVE OWEN

There have been dozens of super-star players for the Giants over the years: lineman Mel Hein, QB Charlie Conerly, RB/WR Frank Gifford, LB Lawrence Taylor, RB Tiki Barber. But we're giving our *ultimate* nod to the coach from 1931–1953. Owen led the team to two NFL titles and later made the Hall of Fame.

FUNKY FACTS

→ Before moving into their current home, the Giants played in baseball stadiums, including the Polo Grounds and Yankee Stadium.

→ A simple kneel-down by QB Joe Pisarcik would have ended a 1978 game. Instead, he tried to hand off, fumbled, and watched the Eagles go for a game-winning touchdown!

→ We don't mean to quibble, but the Giants haven't played in New York City since 1975! They play their home games in New Jersey at Giants Stadium.

→ Don't make plans in January, Giants fans. Your team has made

SUPERSTAR!
ELI MANNING

After being booed early in his pro career, Manning rocketed to the top during the 2007 playoffs. His late-game heroics helped to carry the Giants to a Super Bowl championship!

the playoffs 30 times in its history, the most of any NFL team.

→ If you ever see this team called the "Jints," it's not bad spelling—it's a local nickname!

You Can Look It Up! THE GIANTS' OFFICIAL WEBSITE: www.giants.com

PHILADELPHIA EAGLES

The Eagles have thrilled their fans over the years, winning championships and fielding superstars. Recent seasons have ended in frustration, though, with losses in four NFC Championship Games since 2001.

GAME 1?
1933

When Philly's Frankford Yellow Jackets folded in 1931, a spot opened up for a new NFL team. A group led by Bert Bell paid the NFL $2,500 for the right to found the Eagles.

 ## MAGIC MOMENT
Last Time on Top

In the years before the Super Bowl, the NFL Championship Game was the *ultimate* goal. The Eagles beat the Packers in the 1960 finale.

 ## LOWEST LOW
Bad All Over

The Eagles had the worst offense *and* the worst defense in the NFL in 1937. How'd they manage to win two games?

STUFF

HOME:
Lincoln Financial Field

SUPER BOWL TITLES: 0

ONLY IN PHILLY:
How tough are football fans in Philly? A man dressed as Santa came to a game—and fans booed and threw snowballs at him!

STAR SEASONS!

1949 The Eagles beat the Rams to win their second NFL title in a row.

1987 Defensive end Reggie White led the NFL with 21 sacks. To prove it wasn't a fluke, he led the league again in 1988 with 18.

2007 All-around star Brian Westbrook led the NFL with 2,104 yards from scrimmage (combined rushing and receiving yards).

The Ultimate Eagle
CHUCK BEDNARIK

Lots of players are all-stars at one position. Only a small handful were superstars at two! Chuck "Concrete Charlie" Bednarik was an All-Pro center and also one of the hardest-hitting linebackers ever. He played almost every minute of the 1960 NFL Championship Game to cap a Hall-of-Fame career.

FUNKY FACTS

➔ Great news, Philly! You get the first pick in the brand-new NFL Draft in 1936. Bad news! The player you pick, Heisman-winner Jay Berwanger, decides to skip pro football and go into business.

➔ Because World War II service took so many players, the Eagles merged with the Pittsburgh Steelers in 1943 to form the "Steagles."

➔ QB Randall Cunningham could do it all. For Philly, he led NFL QBs in rushing five times, ran for 32 TDs, and even punted a dozen times!

SUPERSTAR!
BRIAN WESTBROOK

Running, catching, even throwing touchdowns! Westbrook has been a mainstay of the Philly offense since 2002. His soft hands and breakaway speed make him a multipurpose threat.

➔ Lucky fans at Eagles games can enter a contest to be the "sidekick" of the team mascot, Swoop. The winners get to wear mini-Swoop costumes and cheer for the team from the sidelines.

You Can Look It Up! PHILADELPHIA'S OFFICIAL WEBSITE: www.philadelphiaeagles.com

WASHINGTON
REDSKINS

At home in our nation's capital, the Redskins are one of the oldest and most successful NFL teams. Presidents have been big fans over the years, but the most loyal 'Skins fans come from Virginia, Maryland, and Delaware!

GAME 1?
1932

The team started out as the Boston Braves in 1932, became the Redskins in 1933, and moved to Washington, D.C., in 1937. George Preston Marshall owned the team from 1932–1969.

 ## MAGIC MOMENT
Super Bowl XXVI

Washington whipped Buffalo 37–24 to win its third Super Bowl. They became the fourth team to take home a trio of trophies.

 ## LOWEST LOW
A Record Loss

The Redskins suffered the worst loss in NFL history. In the 1940 NFL Championship Game, the Bears beat them . . . 73–0!

STUFF

HOME:
FedExField

SUPER BOWL TITLES: **3**

ONLY IN D.C.:
Washington fans sing one of the most famous fight songs in pro sports, "Hail to the Redskins!"

STAR SEASONS!

1943 In the days when guys played both offense and defense, Sammy Baugh led the NFL in passing, punting, and pickoffs.

1983 Running back John Riggins set an NFL record (since broken) with 24 touchdowns.

1984 Receiver Art Monk set a then-NFL record with 106 catches. He would later set a record with a catch in 183 straight games.

The Ultimate Redskin
DARRELL GREEN

Many great offensive stars have worn Redskins burgundy and gold, but a defender gets our vote for the *ultimate* 'Skin. He excelled at defensive back for 20 years. He was one of the fastest players in NFL history, too! This Hall of Famer picked off 54 passes and was chosen for seven Pro Bowls.

FUNKY FACTS

➜ Redskins owner George Marshall was a pioneer. Not only did he hire the first NFL team band, he encouraged new rules that led to higher scoring and was the first to put his team on TV regularly. Regrettably, Marshall was opposed to hiring African American players, and his team was the last to do so, in 1963.

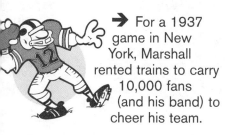

➜ For a 1937 game in New York, Marshall rented trains to carry 10,000 fans (and his band) to cheer his team.

➜ Washington's Mark Moseley was the last non-soccer-style kicker in the NFL. He was named NFL MVP in 1982 for scoring 161 points.

SUPERSTAR!
CLINTON PORTIS

With five seasons of 1,300-plus rushing yards, including a team-record 1,516 in 2005, Portis has been one of the best running backs of the past decade. He's the key to the Washington offense.

➜ When were the Redskins the Smurfs? That was the nickname for an early 1980s group of undersized Washington receivers. No, they were not blue.

You Can Look It Up! WASHINGTON'S OFFICIAL WEB SITE: www.redskins.com

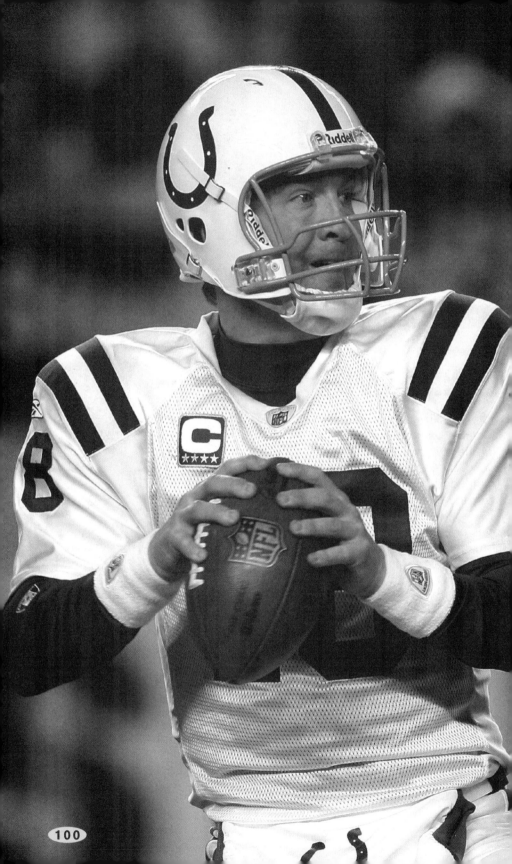

FOURTH
QUARTER

The clock is ticking down to zero . . . your team is trailing . . . who do you call? The quarterback! It's hero time! Let's meet the top passers in NFL history, the all-time greats who stand tall in the huddle and long in our memories. You'll read about these quarterbacks' most memorable feats—and about the coaches who guided them to superstardom.

INSIDE:

Peyton Manning can't wait to read this chapter!

PASSING FANCY

They're the stars. The heroes. The guys who make all the commercials and get all the attention. Of course, when their team loses, they get all the blame, too. They're the quarterbacks, and they play what is possibly the hardest and most pressure-packed position in all of sports. Still, as tough as the job is, some players have excelled at it. Here's a look at the QBs at the top of the important statistical categories.

CAREER TOUCHDOWN PASSES

Brett **Favre***	464
Dan **Marino**	420
Fran **Tarkenton**	342
Peyton **Manning***	333
John **Elway**	300

TOUCHDOWN PASSES, SINGLE SEASON

Tom **Brady**, Patriots	**50** (2007)
Peyton **Manning**, Colts	**49** (2004)
Dan **Marino**, Dolphins	**48** (1984)
Dan **Marino**, Dolphins	**44** (1986)
Kurt **Warner**, Rams	**41** (1999)

CAREER PASSING YARDS

Brett **Favre***   65,127

Dan **Marino**   61,361

John **Elway**   51,475

Warren **Moon**   49,325

Fran **Tarkenton**   47,003

PASSING YARDS, SINGLE SEASON

Dan **Marino**, Dolphins   **5,084** (1984)

Drew **Brees**, Saints   **5,069** (2008)

Kurt **Warner**, Rams   **4,830** (2001)

Tom **Brady**, Patriots   **4,806** (2007)

Dan **Fouts**, Chargers   **4,802** (1981)

CAREER PASSER RATING

Steve **Young**   96.8

Peyton **Manning*** 94.7

Tony **Romo***   94.7

Kurt **Warner***   93.8

Tom **Brady***   92.9

*Active through 2008.

WHAT'S A PASSER RATING?

In 1973, the NFL came up with a complicated math formula to compare QBs. Basically, it takes a few key stats, puts them into a blender, and spits out a single number. A "perfect" passer rating is 158.3. A good rating is around 90 or 100. The season record is 121.1, set by the Colts' Peyton Manning in 2004.

QB HEROES

Thanks to powerful passing arms, terrific teammates, and sometimes just plain guts, a handful of quarterbacks have become legends. These are the players to whom all QBs are compared, the men whose deeds will forever inspire awe. Let's meet our all-time top five.

Sammy Baugh

Baugh was the NFL's first great passing threat. He was known as "Slingin'" Sammy not for his football arm, but for how well he threw a baseball. Baugh grew up in Texas and played in college at Texas Christian University. He played with the Washington Redskins from 1937 to 1952. When the T-formation changed how offenses worked in the 1940s, he was the first passer to take advantage. He led the league in passing six times. On "Sammy Baugh Day" in 1947, he threw six touchdown passes!

Otto Graham

In ten seasons with the Cleveland Browns, "Automatic Otto" led his team to ten championship games. Now *that's* a career! In 1946, Coach Paul Brown convinced Graham to sign with the Browns, a team in the upstart All-America Football Conference. Together, they created a dynasty. They won four AAFC titles and then joined the NFL in 1950 . . . and kept winning! By the time he retired in 1955, Graham had led the Browns to an amazing seven championships.

Johnny Unitas

The *ultimate* QB, Unitas was a great passer, a tough runner, an inspiring leader, and an innovator on offense. He was cut by the Pittsburgh Steelers in 1955 and was playing for a semipro team when the Colts called in 1956. He ended up leading them until 1972. Under Unitas, the Colts won the 1958 and 1959 NFL titles, and also Super Bowl V. When he retired, he was the all-time leader in every major passing category.

Joe Montana

They called him "Joe Cool" because nothing could bother him. No game was too big for him to win, no defense too fierce to overcome. When time was running out and your team needed a score, you wanted Montana in the huddle. He was not the biggest QB ever, nor the fastest, nor did he have the strongest arm. He just made plays and won games. He won three Super Bowl MVPs while leading the 49ers to four NFL titles in the 1980s. He later joined the Chiefs and led them to the playoffs, too.

Brett Favre

Quarterbacks take a lot of hits in the NFL. Few QBs are tough enough–or lucky enough–to even make every start in a season. But Brett Favre started an amazing 269 straight games between 1992 and 2008. And he was as spectacular as he was dependable. Favre turned around a poor Packers team and made it a Super Bowl champion. Along the way, he broke just about every major career passing record.

JUST BELOW THE TOP

There is that pantheon of greatness (which means "list of great guys") that includes names such as Baugh, Montana, and Unitas. But just below them are another stretch of passing heroes worth knowing. Here's our take on some QBs who are among the all-time best. Some are players you've met earlier, so we won't write as much about them here.

Terry Bradshaw

His powerful arm led the Steelers to four Super Bowl titles.

Tom Brady

This Patriots hero had earned three Super Bowl rings by age 27.

John Elway

An expert at last-minute comebacks, he carried Denver to five Super Bowls.

Dan Fouts

This rocket-armed passer topped 4,000 yards in three different seasons.

Peyton Manning

A passer, a leader, a (Super Bowl) winner, a three-time NFL MVP.

Dan Marino
Record-setting passer with
the quickest release ever.

Warren Moon
A star in Canada and the U.S.
and an African American QB pioneer.

Fran Tarkenton
Perfected the art of the scramble
and threw for 47,003 yards.

Steve Young
Best lefty passer ever, accurate and mobile.

Other Lefties

Here's a list of notable left-handed QBs in
NFL history. They're listed with the team
they played for the longest:

Frankie Albert, 49ers
Mark Brunell, Jaguars
Boomer Esiason, Bengals
Ken Stabler, Raiders
Michael Vick, Falcons
Jim Zorn, Seahawks

IN THE TRENCHES

Every play starts with a center snap and the headlong clash of two large groups of dudes. They are the linemen—offensive and defensive. Butting heads, flailing arms, bumping bellies, they push and shove like elephants in a dance of balance and strength. Let's take a close look at them and their work.

THE POSITIONS

Here are the key positions on the O-line and the D-line (football-speak for the offensive and defensive lines, of course).

Offense

POSITION	WHERE	ACTIONS
Center	center of line	calls signals for linemen, snaps ball to QB, blocks
Guards	next to center	blocks
Tackles	next to guards	blocks
Tight end	outside tackle	blocks and catches passes

Defense

Nose tackle	opposite center	tackles guy with ball
Defensive tackles	near center of line	tackles guy with ball
Defensive ends	opposite tackles	tackles guy with ball

THE LINGO

Players on the line of scrimmage have their own language. Here are some words you might hear just before you end up at the bottom of a couple of tons of padded human being.

BLIND SIDE: a quarterback's back side. A righty, for instance, can't see someone charging up behind him on his left.

HOLE: space created by offensive linemen for runners to slip through.

POCKET: the area formed by the blockers from which a quarterback can pass safely.

PULL: when a lineman leads the way around the end for a runner.

STUNT: a move in which D-linemen cross paths to confuse blockers.

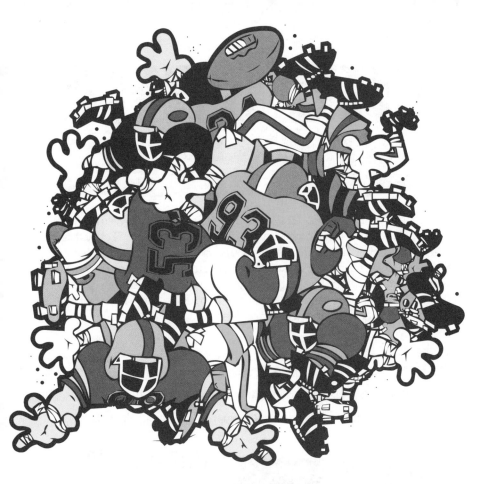

THE STARS

Blockers don't get much attention, so let's give them some now. Ladies and gentlemen, boys and girls, the best offensive linemen of all time!

CENTERS:
❖ **Bulldog Turner,** Bears ❖ **Mel Hein,** Giants
❖ **Jim Otto,** Raiders ❖ **Dwight Stephenson,** Dolphins
❖ **Mike Webster,** Steelers

GUARDS:
❖ **Dan Fortmann,** Bears ❖ **Gene Upshaw,** Raiders
❖ **Ron Mix,** Chargers ❖ **John Hannah,** Patriots

TACKLES:
❖ **Roosevelt Brown,** Giants ❖ **Forrest Gregg,** Packers
❖ **Jim Parker,** Colts ❖ **Art Shell,** Raiders
❖ **Anthony Muñoz,** Bengals ❖ **Jonathan Ogden,** Ravens

THE GREAT COACHES

Coaches in the NFL are among the most powerful people in sports. They are in charge of the entire team. They have to make hundreds of decisions each week: which men to play, which plays to run, what to serve at dinner the night before the game, what music to play on the bus ride to the stadium. It's a demanding job! Here are some of the men who have done the job better than the rest.

PAUL BROWN Coached Cleveland Browns to three NFL titles . . . first coach to use a playbook, film study, player grades, and in-depth scouting reports . . . later, first coach and owner of Cincinnati Bengals.

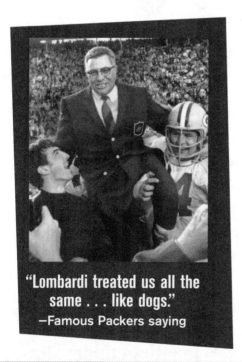

"Lombardi treated us all the same . . . like dogs."
—Famous Packers saying

GEORGE HALAS Owned Chicago Bears for 60 years . . . head coach for 40 years . . . won six NFL titles . . . perfected use of T-formation on offense . . . also played for Bears in 1920s.

CURLY LAMBEAU Founded Green Bay Packers in 1919 and coached them until 1949 . . . won six NFL championships . . . helped spur popularity of passing offense in late 1930s . . . also played halfback in 1920s.

MADDEN!

You've heard of John Madden, right? He's the guy whose name is on that enormously popular video game. Guess what? He was once an NFL coach! Before Madden got famous talking football on TV and then helping to design the video game, he ran a football team. He led the Oakland Raiders from 1969–1978. They even won a Super Bowl for him in 1976. He stopped coaching because he didn't like flying around the country. From 1979–2009, he helped TV viewers understand the plays they were watching . . . when they weren't playing video games, that is.

VINCE LOMBARDI

Greatest football coach ever . . . led Packers in 1960s to five NFL titles . . . famously tough . . . Super Bowl trophy named in his honor.

TOM LANDRY

Led Dallas Cowboys for 29 years . . . guided them to 20 straight winning seasons and two Super Bowl wins . . . created new offensive strategies . . . popularized "Shotgun" formation and invented the 4-3 defense.

DON SHULA

All-time leader in coaching wins with 347 . . . led Colts and then Dolphins . . . under Shula, Miami won two Super Bowls . . . Dolphins' 1972 team went 17-0, only undefeated, untied team ever.

BILL WALSH

Creator of so-called "West Coast Offense" focusing on quick timing passes, which are still popular today . . . led 49ers to three Super Bowl wins in 1980s (team won a fourth the year after he left) . . . more than a dozen of his former assistant coaches have gone on to become head coaches.

ANY GIVEN SUNDAY

One of the most famous sayings in the NFL is, "On any given Sunday, any team can be a winner." Just because a team is mighty, powerful, and talented doesn't mean it can't lose. After you read about these upsets, think of them the next time you're facing a scary math test.

1950 BROWNS OVER EAGLES For their first game in the NFL, the Browns were matched against the Eagles, the defending NFL champs. Though the Browns had won the AAFC title a year earlier, few thought Cleveland had a chance. But the Browns grounded the Eagles, winning 35–10.

1968 JETS OVER COLTS Experts thought the AFL's Jets would lose Super Bowl III to the mighty NFL Colts by at least 17 points! Until then, an AFL team had never beaten an NFL team. Jets QB Joe Namath boldly "guaranteed" that his team would win . . . and they did. It was the most important upset in league history.

1995 PANTHERS OVER 49ERS The Panthers were in their first season—ever! The 49ers were the defending Super Bowl champs! It should have been a Niners rout. Instead, the Panthers D throttled the Niners' powerful offense. A 96-yard interception-return TD was the key to the Panthers' 13–7 upset win—in San Francisco!

1996 JAGUARS OVER BILLS/BRONCOS The Jaguars were just two years old in 1996, but they won six of their last seven games and squeezed into the playoffs. Then the *real* surprises came in the next two weeks. First they kicked a late field goal to upset Buffalo 30–27. A week later, they beat Denver, the season's top team, by the same score.

2007 GIANTS OVER PATRIOTS The New England Patriots had not lost a game all season. They boasted the best QB in the game in Tom Brady. They had rolled through the playoffs with ease. The Giants, on the other hand, were somewhat of a surprise to reach Super Bowl XLII. But thanks to a miracle play in the final minute (see page 130 for more details), the Giants handed New England its only loss of the season—and gave NFL fans a memory for a lifetime.

GREATEST
COMEBACKS

The game "ain't over 'til the fat lady sings," goes the famous saying. (They mean like an opera singer.) Great teams know that as long as there is time left on the clock, there's a chance to come back and win. Here are the NFL's greatest comebacks.

POINTS BEHIND	WINNER	LOSER	SEASON
32	**Bills**	**Oilers**	**1992**

The greatest comeback ever! And it came in a wild-card playoff game. The Bills were behind 35–3, led 38–35, saw it tied again at 38–38, and then won in overtime 41–38.

28	**49ers**	**Saints**	**1980**

Down by four TDs? No problem, as long as Joe Montana is your QB. The Niners rallied with 31 unanswered points in the second half and overtime to create the best regular-season comeback ever.

26	**Bills**	**Colts**	**1997**

Three fourth-quarter TDs, including a 54-yard rushing score, helped the Bills come back to win. They had to prevent a two-point conversion with less than a minute left to seal their comeback.

MORE COMEBACK STORIES

* Frank Reich, the QB who led the Bills to their 1992 comeback, also led the University of Maryland to a 31-point comeback over the University of Miami. That's the best ever by a college team.

* Ten NFL teams have come from 24 points behind to win. The most recent was in 1992, when the Rams rallied from a 27–3 deficit to defeat the Buccaneers.

* The second-biggest playoff comeback was in the 2002 season, when the 49ers scored eight points in the third quarter and 17 in the fourth to bounce back from a 24-point deficit and nip the Giants 39–38.

CHICAGO BEARS

Da Bears! As one of the NFL's most storied teams, the Bears boast a rich history, loyal fans, monsters, a Refrigerator, Sweetness, and a famous rap video. When you've been playing for more than 80 years, a lot can happen!

GAME 1?
1920

The Decatur Staleys were one of the NFL's original teams. In 1922, they became the Chicago Bears . . . and that's what they've been ever since.

 ## MAGIC MOMENT
Super Bowl XX

After putting together one of the most dominant seasons in NFL history, the 1985 Bears wiped the floor with the Patriots, winning 46–10.

 ## LOWEST LOW
Bad Moves

In 1969, the final year before the NFL merged with the AFL, the Bears won only one game. Good thing the NFL still took them!

STUFF

HOME:
Soldier Field

SUPER BOWL TITLES: 1

ONLY IN CHICAGO:
A little weather doesn't bother Bears fans. In 2008, more than 62,000 came when it was a record-low of 2° F!

STAR SEASONS!

1977 Walter "Sweetness" Payton led the NFL with a team record of 1,852 rushing yards. (He retired in 1987 as the NFL's all-time leader.)

1985 Defensive end Richard Dent led the NFL with 17 sacks, and the Bears set the (since-broken) record for fewest points allowed in a 16-game season (198).

2007 Devin Hester returned four punts and two kickoffs for TDs.

The Ultimate Bear
GEORGE HALAS

The man they called "Papa Bear" was a part of the team for more than 60 years. Halas was a player, a coach, the owner, and the general manager. Halas first led the team to an NFL title in 1921. His last championship as a coach came in 1963! He was one of the first members of the Hall of Fame.

FUNKY FACTS

➜ Though the Bears have won only one Super Bowl, they did win eight other NFL championships in the pre-Super Bowl era.

➜ One of the team's nicknames: Monsters of the Midway, referring to a park area in Chicago.

➜ The 1985 Bears were so cocky that they made their famous "Super Bowl Shuffle" video three weeks before the playoffs even began!

➜ In Super Bowl XX, an oversized defensive tackle named William "The Refrigerator" Perry scored a touchdown on a one-yard plunge. It felt like an earthquake!

SUPERSTAR!
MATT FORTÉ

Running back Matt Forté was only a rookie in 2008, but he put up veteran numbers. Strong and quick, Forté scored 12 touchdowns and ran for 1,238 yards.

➜ In the 1940 NFL Championship Game, the Bears put a record whipping on Washington, winning 73–0. That's still the most points ever scored in one game by an NFL team!

You Can Look It Up! CHICAGO'S OFFICIAL WEBSITE: www.chicagobears.com

DETROIT LIONS

The Lions hit bottom in 2008 (see "Lowest Low") but that means the only way to go is up! Their history includes some great teams and great players. Their fans are hoping that history will repeat itself (just not 2008!).

GAME 1?
1930

Their fans used to say "Go Spartans!" From 1930–1933, the team was the Portsmouth (Mich.) Spartans. They moved to Detroit and took their current name in 1934.

 ## MAGIC MOMENT
Their Last Title

Let's go all the way back to 1957 to find a real magic moment, when the Lions beat the Browns 59–14 in the NFL Championship Game.

 ## LOWEST LOW
Duh!

The easiest lowest low to pick in the book. In 2008, the Lions became the first team ever to go (gulp!) 0–16.

STUFF

HOME:
Ford Field

SUPER BOWL TITLES: **0**

ONLY IN DETROIT:
Playing on Thanksgiving Day is a tradition that goes all the way back to 1934, the team's first season in Detroit.

STAR SEASONS!

1935 Led by future Hall of Famer Dutch Clark, the Lions won their first NFL title in only their sixth season, knocking off the Giants.

1995 Receiver Herman Moore caught a then-record 123 passes.

1997 Swivel-hipped Barry Sanders ran for an NFL-leading 2,053 yards, now the third-highest single-season total ever.

The Ultimate Lion

BOBBY LAYNE

Okay, so he hasn't played in Detroit since 1958. He is still the team's all-time leader in passing yards. He also guided the Lions to NFL championships in 1952, 1953, and 1957. Layne was a tough-guy QB, not afraid to run with the ball and take a hit. In 1967, he was elected to the Hall of Fame.

FUNKY FACTS

➔ Buddy Parker coached the Lions to two NFL titles, but he quit without warning two days before the first preseason game in 1957. New coach George Wilson did okay on short notice, though. He led the team to the league championship!

➔ Alex Karras was a star defensive tackle for the Lions, mostly in the 1960s. Movie buffs, though, know him as the man who punched a horse in the comedy *Blazing Saddles*.

➔ Legendary QB Bobby Layne was traded suddenly in 1958. He supposedly put a curse on the Lions, saying "They won't win again for 50 years." Exactly 50 years later, they went 0–16!

SUPERSTAR!

CALVIN JOHNSON

The play of this speedy, sure-handed, second-year receiver was a rare bright spot in the Lions' tough 2008 season. Johnson caught 12 TDs and was among NFC leaders with 1,331 receiving yards.

➔ Wanna hear something weird? The Lions' record in the 2008 preseason, before they went 0–16 in the regular season, was a perfect 4–0!

You Can Look It Up! DETROIT'S OFFICIAL WEBSITE: www.detroitlions.com

GREEN BAY
PACKERS

Almost nothing says "NFL" like the Green Bay Packers. From the legendary coaching of Lambeau and Lombardi, to the recent superstardom of Brett Favre, Packers history has been one long tale of football greatness.

GAME 1?
1921

The NFL was only a year old (and wasn't even called the NFL yet—see page 10) when the Packers joined. The team had actually been playing since 1919, just not in the NFL.

MAGIC MOMENT
Super Bowl XXXI

After a long dry spell, the Packers returned to the top of the NFL, winning their third Super Bowl by defeating the Patriots 35–21.

LOWEST LOW
Pre-Vince

The season before coach Vince Lombardi took over was a real low point for the Pack. The 1958 team won only one game!

STUFF

HOME:
Lambeau Field

SUPER BOWL TITLES: **3**

ONLY IN GREEN BAY:
Packers fans often wear giant yellow foam wedges on their heads. Why? Their nickname— the Cheeseheads!

STAR SEASONS!

1942 Don Hutson led the NFL in catches, receiving yards, and touchdowns. His 74 receptions trounced the guy in second place, who caught a measly 27.

1996 Brett Favre threw 39 touchdown passes, setting a new team record and leading the NFL.

2003 Running back Ahman Green set a Packers record by rushing for 1,883 yards.

The Ultimate Packer
BRETT FAVRE

A trade with the Falcons landed the Packers the best player in their history. Favre led the team from 1992 through 2007 and never missed a game! Favre was not only a great passer, he was a tremendous leader. He had a great ability for rallying his team from behind late in games.

FUNKY FACTS

→ Green Bay won the first two Super Bowls, then again with XXXI. But they've also won nine other NFL championships. Their total of 12 is the most in the league!

→ Who owns this team? For the Packers, the answer is "the fans." In 1923, Green Bay residents were permitted to buy shares in the team. It is still community owned.

→ The Super Bowl championship trophy was named in honor of Lombardi, following his death from cancer in 1970.

→ The founder of the Packers was Earl "Curly" Lambeau. He was not only

SUPERSTAR!
AARON RODGERS

Aaron Rodgers had some big cleats to fill when he became the Packers QB in 2008. In his first season as a starter, Rodgers put up Favre-like numbers: 4,038 passing yards and 28 TDs.

the coach for 29 years, he also was a player for nine!

→ It gets so cold in Green Bay that the field has heating pipes so that the grass won't freeze solid!

You Can Look It Up! GREEN BAY'S OFFICIAL WEBSITE: www.packers.com

MINNESOTA VIKINGS

They play in a giant bubble, they've never won it all, and they wear purple. Still, the Vikings have fielded some fine teams and many outstanding players. With young stars such as A.P. on their side, their future is bright.

GAME 1?
1961

The Vikings joined the NFL as an expansion team for the 1961 season. The league let them pick some second-string players from other teams and sign some rookies.

 ## MAGIC MOMENT
Game On!

The Vikings got off to a great start in their first-ever game. Their young players and castoffs beat the mighty Bears 37–13.

 ## LOWEST LOW
Thiiiiis Close in '98

Gary Anderson flubbed a 38-yard FG try, costing the Vikings a trip to the Super Bowl. And it was his first miss all season!

STUFF

HOME:
The Metrodome

SUPER BOWL TITLES: **0**

ONLY IN MINNESOTA:
Look for Ragnar the Viking at Minnesota games, dressed in furs and a horned helmet and riding an un-Viking-like motorcycle.

STAR SEASONS!

1969 QB Joe Kapp threw for a record seven touchdowns in one game during the Vikings' march to Super Bowl IV.

1998 Receiver Randy Moss set a rookie record—and led the NFL—with 17 touchdown catches.

2004 QB Daunte Culpepper led the NFL and set a Vikings record by racking up 4,717 passing yards.

The Ultimate Viking
JIM MARSHALL

We could have chosen any of several members of the famed Purple People Eaters defense–Alan Page, Carl Eller, Paul Krause. But we'll give the foam tribute to a 20-year veteran defensive tackle. When Marshall retired in 1979, he had played in a then-record 282 NFL games.

#1

FUNKY FACTS

→ Longtime coach Bud Grant was a pretty good athlete. Not only did he play pro football, he was in the NBA for a while, with the Lakers. He also coached in the Canadian Football League.

→ The Vikings defense in the 1970s had one of the great nicknames in sports: "The Purple People Eaters." The nickname actually came from a popular song.

→ The Vikings were the first team to lose four Super Bowls. The Buffalo Bills and Denver Broncos later joined this unhappy club.

→ Though Jim Marshall is our *ultimate* Viking, he's also an *ultimate*

SUPERSTAR!
ADRIAN PETERSON

In only two seasons, the man they call "A.P." has become one of the NFL's best players. After setting a single-game rushing record as a rookie in 2007, he led the NFL with 1,760 yards in 2008.

Goof-up. In a 1964 game, he picked up a fumble and returned it to the end zone. One problem: he had run the wrong way! The other team was given a two-point safety thanks to Marshall. Oops.

You Can Look It Up! MINNESOTA'S OFFICIAL WEBSITE: www.vikings.com

SUPER BOWL!

Go, Harrison, go! Super Bowl XLIII in February 2009 was an awesome game. But it was just the 43rd in a long line of amazing, historic Super Bowls. In this chapter, you'll catch passes from Kurt Warner, kick game-winning field goals, and help search for Thurman Thomas's helmet. Get ready to hoist that big silver trophy!

INSIDE:

Pittsburgh's James Harrison runs right into Super Bowl history!

IN THE BEGINNING ...

Did you know there was once a time when there was no Super Bowl? We're not talking about, like, during the American Revolution or something. We mean as recently as when your teachers were kids! The first Super Bowl was not played until after the 1966 season. Here are some facts about the birth of the biggest game in sports!

The Origin

In 1960, the American Football League was formed. It was a rival for the older, more popular National Football League. For a while, the NFL didn't pay much attention. Then the AFL started signing great college players. It got its games on TV. Some fans started supporting AFL teams instead of NFL teams. In 1966, the two leagues decided that joining forces was better than fighting each other. They agreed to "merge," or combine, beginning in 1970. But in the meantime, they each still crowned champions. Those two champs would play each other, it was decided, in an annual championship game.

THE NAME

The first two Super Bowls were not called Super Bowls! They were known as (take a deep breath) "The AFL-NFL World Championship Game." Then Kansas City Chiefs owner Lamar Hunt saw one of his kids playing with an ultra-bouncy "super ball." He thought that might, with a slight change, make a good name for the new big game. The Super Bowl (always two words, please!) was born.

THE TROPHY

Winners of the Super Bowl take home a giant silver football on a tall, triangular base. A new one is made every year for the owner of the winning team. In 1970, the trophy was named the Vince Lombardi Trophy, in honor of the great Packers coach.

THE FIRST GAME

The Green Bay Packers had already won four NFL titles in the 1960s. Playing against the champs of the newer, younger AFL seemed sort of a waste of time. Everyone knew that the Packers would win. But play the game they did, and it turned out like everyone thought: Packers 35, Chiefs 10. Packers receiver Max McGee caught two TD passes. QB Bart Starr was the MVP. (Starr won again the next year.)

Then and Now

	SUPER BOWL I	SUPER BOWL XLIII
Ticket price	$10	$800
Winner's prize	$15,000	$78,000
Avg. NFL salary	$20,000	$1.4 million
No. of NFL teams	15	32

THE SUPER BOWL

SINGLE-GAME RECORDS

Kurt Warner owns the top three single-game passing marks.

MOST TD PASSES, 6

Steve Young,
49ERS
Super Bowl XXIX

MOST PASSING YARDS: 414

Kurt Warner, RAM
Super Bowl XXXIV

MOST RUSHING YARDS: 204

Timmy Smith,
REDSKINS
Super Bowl XXII

MOST RECEIVING YARDS: 215

Jerry Rice, 49ERS
Super Bowl XXIII

MOST RUSHING TDS: 3

Terrell Davis,
BRONCOS
Super Bowl XXXII

MOST INTERCEPTIONS: 3

Rod Martin,
OAKLAND
Super Bowl XV

Other Stuff

Check out these other single-game Super Bowl records:

Most Sacks: 3
Reggie White, Packers, XXXI
Darnell Dockett, Cardinals, XLIII

Most Interceptions Thrown: 5
Rich Gannon, Oakland, XXXVII

Longest Field Goal: 54 yards
Steve Christie, Buffalo, XXVIII

Longest Punt Return: 45 yards
John Taylor, 49ers, XXIII

RECORD BOOK

CAREER RECORDS

MOST TD PASSES: **11**

Joe Montana, 49ERS
Four Super Bowls

MOST PASSING YARDS: **1,156**
Kurt Warner, RAMS/
CARDINALS
Three Super Bowls

MOST RUSHING YARDS: **354**
Franco Harris, STEELERS ▼
Four Super Bowls

MOST TDS: **8**
Jerry Rice,
49ERS/RAIDERS
Four Super Bowls

MOST SACKS: **4.5**
Charles Haley,
49ERS/COWBOYS
Five Super Bowls

MOST RECEIVING YARDS: **589**
Jerry Rice,
49ERS/RAIDERS
Four Super Bowls

MR. SUPER BOWL

Mike Lodish, a defensive lineman, played in six Super Bowls, the most ever. He went four times with Buffalo and twice with Denver.

Franco Harris helped Pittsburgh win four Super Bowls.

HALFTIME
REPORT

THE EARLY DAYS
The first Super Bowl halftime shows were nothing special. A marching band or two. A bunch of people in matching sweaters singing dumb songs (the group Up With People appeared four times!). Finally, in the early 1990s, the NFL realized that it had this massive audience . . . and that boring stuff was not cutting it anymore. So the NFL turned to the biggest stars in music to spice things up. And those stars came through like Joe Montana and Ben Roethlisberger! Here are some highlights from the wildest Super Bowl halftime shows.

ICE SKATING?
In 1992, the Super Bowl was held in a northern city—Minneapolis—for the first time. The game was played at the indoor Metrodome, but the NFL brought a little bit of winter inside. Olympic figure skaters Dorothy Hamill and Brian Boitano performed on a special sheet of ice-like plastic rolled onto the field.

MICHAEL JACKSON
At Super Bowl XXVII at the Rose Bowl, Michael Jackson sang with more than 3,500 kids on the field. At the end of his show, the entire stadium did massive card stunts.

SNAKES?
Giant snakes were part of the halftime show for XXIX. Okay, they weren't real snakes . . . but they were part of an act that had "Indiana Jones" running around trying to "recapture" the Super Bowl trophy.

DIANA ROSS

The NFL had to get special permission from the government for this stunt at Super Bowl XXX in Phoenix. At the end of her show, singer Diana Ross climbed onboard a helicopter, which rose out of the stadium as the crowd went nuts.

U2

New Orleans saw a super show for XXXVI. The NFL brought in rock 'n' royalty for the first time, and the Irish band played a three-song mini-concert.

ROCK LEGENDS

From 2005–2008, the NFL kept the party going with awesome superstar acts year after year. Paul McCartney (the famous former Beatle), Prince, the Rolling Stones, and Tom Petty and the Heartbreakers all rocked the house, er . . . stadium.

BRUCE SPRINGSTEEN

Nothing fancy here, folks. Just a big-time rock 'n' roll god playing some of his favorite songs. Thousands of dancers packed the field at Super Bowl XLIII, waving lights and singing along. What a party!

WHAT A PLAY!

We could do a whole book on the Super Bowl, but we've only got this chapter. So we'll use this page to highlight the biggest plays in the game's history.

O'Brien's Kick (V)

Colts rookie Jim O'Brien makes a winning 32-yard FG in the final seconds.

Swann's Catch (X)

Steelers WR Lynn Swann makes an incredible, diving, falling catch.

Riggins's Rumble (XVII)

On a key fourth-down play, Washington RB John Riggins bursts through the line and scores a go-ahead 43-yard TD.

Allen's Run (XVIII)

Raiders RB pulls off a 74-yard twisting, field-wandering TD run.

Fridge in the End Zone! (XX)

The Bears' William "The Refrigerator" Perry shifts from defensive tackle to TD-scoring fullback . . . and national hero!

The Tackle (XXXIV)

Rams LB Mike Jones saves his team with a last-second tackle at the goal line.

Vinatieri's Kicks (XXXVI and XXXVIII)

Patriots K Adam Vinatieri wins two Super Bowls with last-second field goals.

The Helmet Catch (XLII)

Giants WR David Tyree makes a miracle catch against his helmet to set up the game-winning TD.

SUPER BOWL XLIII:
CAN YOU TOP THIS?

The Steelers' historic 27–23 win over the Cardinals in February 2009 featured three plays that are among the best and biggest ever! Let's take a look back.

Harrison's Hurry-Up

With seconds left in the first half, Arizona was just yards away from taking the lead. But then Pittsburgh LB James Harrison picked off a Kurt Warner pass and rumbled 100 yards for the touchdown as time expired. It was the longest play of any kind in Super Bowl history!

Fitzgerald's Flash

With Arizona trailing by four points and less than three minutes to go, things were looking bad for the Cards. Then star receiver Larry Fitzgerald grabbed a pass and sprinted away from the defense. His 64-yard score gave the Cards the lead . . . briefly.

Santonio's Snag ▶▶▶▶▶▶

There were only 42 seconds left. Pittsburgh had six yards to go. They had to score or the Cardinals would pull off the upset victory. Pittsburgh QB Ben Roethlisberger hung in the pocket and looked to his left. Covered. He looked to the center. Nothing. He went to his third choice on the play, Santonio Holmes. The pass to Holmes zipped over three Arizona defenders. Holmes stretched out, kept his toes inbounds, and snagged the ball . . . touchdown! Victory!

SUPER

The Super Bowl is the world's biggest one-day party. And as with most big parties, some pretty crazy stuff has happened. Let's take a look back at the wildest, wackiest, and weirdest moments in the history of football's premier event.

FLYING VIKINGS?

Super Bowl IV: A hot-air balloon carrying a costumed Viking crashed into the stands during a pregame ceremony. No one was injured, although the mascot's pride was hurt a bit. Of course, Minnesota lost the game, too.

WEIRD!

UH, JIM?
Super Bowl V: Just before he had to try a game-winning field goal (see page 130), Jim O'Brien reached down to pull up some grass to toss and test the wind. One problem: The game was played on artificial turf!

STICK TO KICKING, GARO
Super Bowl VII: Miami kicker Garo Yepremian picked up a blocked field goal and tried a desperation heave to save the play. He passed like a linebacker kicks—badly. The ball slipped out of his hand and was returned for a TD.

HEADBAND HYSTERIA
Super Bowl XX: NFL commissioner Pete Rozelle told Bears QB Jim McMahon not to wear a headband with a sponsor's name. McMahon obeyed. During the game before this Super Bowl, his headband said "Rozelle."

THURMAN'S LOST HELMET
XXVI: What would be a bad day (another Super Bowl loss) started out even worse for Bills RB Thurman Thomas. He missed the team's first two plays because someone had misplaced his helmet!

EARLY CELEBRATION
XXVII: Big Leon Lett picked up a fumble and seemed headed for a Dallas TD. But Buffalo WR Don Beebe didn't give up. When Lett held out the ball in celebration, a hustling Beebe knocked it away just before the big man crossed the goal line.

BEFORE SUPER BOWL XVIII

"I'd run over my mother to win this game."
—RUSS GRIMM
of the Redskins

"I'd run over Grimm's mother, too."
—MATT MILLEN
of the Raiders

THE WINNERS!

A Whole   Mess of Cool Super Bowl Lists!

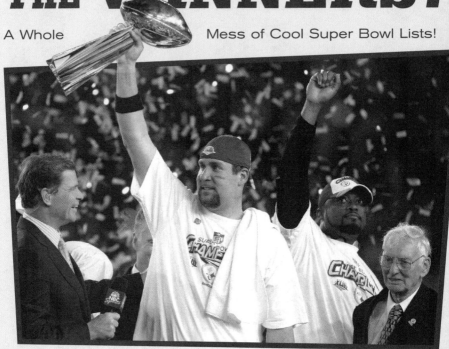

Ben Roethlisberger now plays for the "Sixburgh Steelers."

TEAMS THAT HAVE **WON THE MOST** SUPER BOWLS!

Pittsburgh Steelers **6**

Dallas Cowboys **5**

San Francisco 49ers **5**

Green Bay Packers **3**

New England Patriots **3**

New York Giants **3**

Oakland/L.A. Raiders **3**

Washington Redskins **3**

MVPs Here are the ten most recent Super Bowl MVPs.

XLIII **Santonio Holmes,** WR, Steelers

XLII **Eli Manning,** QB, Giants

XLI **Peyton Manning,** QB, Colts

XL **Hines Ward,** WR, Steelers

XXXIX **Deion Branch,** WR, Patriots

XXXVIII **Tom Brady,** QB, Patriots ▶▶▶▶

XXXVII **Dexter Jackson,** S, Buccaneers

XXXVI **Tom Brady,** QB, Patriots

XXXV **Ray Lewis,** LB, Ravens

XXXIV **Kurt Warner,** QB, Rams

SUPER HOME!

These places have hosted the Super Bowl the most times.

Miami/South Florida	**9**
New Orleans	**9**
Los Angeles/Pasadena	**7**
Tampa	**4**
San Diego	**3**

Super Future!

SUPER BOWL XLIV (2010)
Dolphin Stadium (Miami)

SUPER BOWL XLV (2011)
Cowboys Stadium*

SUPER BOWL XLVI (2012)
Lucas Oil Stadium (Indianapolis)
*Stadium name still to be chosen.

ATLANTA
FALCONS

Though they're still looking for their first NFL title, the Falcons have had some bright moments in their history, including a really big bounceback in 2008. With some of the best young talent in the NFL, this is a team to watch.

GAME 1?
1966

The South got its first NFL team (well, first modern team . . . there was a Louisville team briefly in the 1920s) when Atlanta was awarded an expansion franchise.

 ## MAGIC MOMENT
Super Bowl XXXIII

They lost to Denver 34–19, but just making it to the Super Bowl was a huge deal for a team that had struggled for decades.

 ## LOWEST LOW
Slow Start

The Falcons had a tough time learning to fly in the NFL. From 1966–1968, they won only six games and lost 35!

STUFF

HOME:
The Georgia Dome

SUPER BOWL TITLES: 0

ONLY IN ATLANTA:
In 1977, the team's defense gained a nickname—"The Gritz Blitz." It was inspired by a popular Southern dish.

STAR SEASONS!

1977 The Falcons set an NFL record for the fewest points allowed in a 14-game season (129).

1980 Steve Bartkowski, who holds all the team's career passing marks, had his best season, leading the NFL with 31 TD passes.

1998 Jamal Anderson set a team record by rushing for 1,846 yards while helping the Falcons to their only Super Bowl.

JEFF VAN NOTE

The Falcons have had some great stars—QB Steve Bartkowski, RB William Andrews, DE Claude Humphrey—but here we honor a quieter hero. Van Note started at center for the Falcons in nearly every game from 1970 through 1985. He played in five Pro Bowls, too.

FUNKY FACTS

➜ Astronauts hate Falcons. While orbiting Earth in 1966, NASA's finest begged Tommy Nobis to sign with their hometown Houston Oilers. But Atlanta snapped him up and he became a longtime star at linebacker.

➜ In 1998, coach Dan Reeves had major heart surgery. Amazingly, he was back on the sidelines just four weeks later.

➜ Kicker Morten Andersen, who grew up in Denmark, spent eight seasons with Atlanta. His team-leading 806 points are part of an NFL record total of 2,544.

SUPERSTAR! MATT RYAN

It's rare for a quarterback to star in his rookie season. But Ryan did just that, leading the Falcons into the NFL playoffs for the first time since 2004.

➜ The Falcons earned their berth in Super Bowl XXXIII (their only one . . . so far!) by beating the Vikings in the first NFC title game ever to go into overtime.

You Can Look It Up! ATLANTA'S OFFICIAL WEBSITE: www.atlantafalcons.com

CAROLINA
PANTHERS

For such a young team, the Panthers have had a very busy NFL life. In just 14 years, they've played in three NFC Championship Games and one Super Bowl. With a start like that, look out, future!

GAME 1?
1995

The NFL was looking to expand, and it had never had a team in the booming Carolinas. Former NFL receiver Jerry Richardson put together a group that got a new team for North Carolina.

 ## MAGIC MOMENT
Super Bowl XXXVIII

It ended with a disappointing last-second loss, but reaching the Super Bowl was a huge boost for this young team.

 ## LOWEST LOW
Bump in the Road

After winning at least seven games in five of its first six seasons, Carolina plummeted to a 1–15 record in 2001.

STUFF

HOME:
Bank of America Stadium

SUPER BOWL TITLES: 0

ONLY IN CHARLOTTE:
According to his bio, Carolina mascot "Sir Purr" studied "purr-forming arts" at CAT-awba College.

STAR SEASONS!

1999 Veteran QB Steve Beuerlein led the NFL with a team-record 4,436 passing yards. He also threw 36 TD passes.

2005 Steve Smith led the NFL in both receptions (103) and receiving yards (1,563).

2008 DeAngelo Williams joined the ranks of elite NFL runners with a pair of team records: 1,515 yards and 20 total touchdowns.

The Ultimate Panther

JOHN KASAY

The left-footed Kasay is the only full-time kicker in Panthers history. Since joining the expansion team in 1995, he has topped 24 field goals in seven seasons. Kasay is also the team's all-time leader in games played and points scored, and has made a dozen game-winning field goals.

#1

FUNKY FACTS

➔ The Panthers set a new standard for young teams when they made it all the way to the NFC Championship Game in only their second season.

➔ Why not the *North* Carolina Panthers? By keeping the North out, the team tries to appeal to fans in South Carolina, too.

➔ Team owner Jerry Richardson became the first former NFL player (he was a Colts receiver) to be the majority owner of an NFL team. Richardson made his fortune running a fast-food chain.

SUPERSTAR!

STEVE SMITH

Smith doesn't care that he's shorter and lighter than most big-play receivers. He uses his speed and courage to make catch after catch. He has topped 1,000 receiving yards five times!

➔ Good start! The Panthers set a new record for wins by a team in its first season by going 7–9 in 1995.

You Can Look It Up! CAROLINA'S OFFICIAL WEBSITE: www.panthers.com

NEW ORLEANS SAINTS

When you think of long-term poor play, of teams that just can't seem to catch a break, of fans who wear bags on their heads—you think of the Saints. But with a new Brees blowing through town, maybe the good times will roll!

GAME 1?
1967

The Saints joined the NFL as an expansion team during a time that the league was battling with the AFL for fans' attention. Putting a team in a town known for having fun was a great idea!

 MAGIC MOMENT
One Long Kick

In 1970, kicker Tom Dempsey made a record 63-yard field goal to beat the Lions. It's still tied for the longest kick ever in the NFL history.

 LOWEST LOW
Lots of Lows

For a team that went 21 years without a winning season, there are lots to choose from. Let's pick the worst: 1980, with a 1–15 finish.

STUFF

HOME:
Louisiana Superdome

SUPER BOWL TITLES: **0**

ONLY IN NEW ORLEANS:
Fans used to celebrating Mardi Gras often come to games decked out in party beads and wild costumes.

STAR SEASONS!

1969 Danny Abramowicz was an early star for the Saints, leading the NFL with 73 receptions.

1991 As part of the feared "Dome Patrol," LB Pat Swilling led the NFL with 17 sacks.

2008 Strong-armed QB Drew Brees (see "Superstar!") set a team record while leading the NFL with 34 TD passes.

The Ultimate Saint

ARCHIE MANNING

Archie Manning led the Saints to 35 victories! Unfortunately, it took him ten years. However, his solid play amid a team of, well, not-very-good players earned him the respect and love of Saints fans. Today's fans, though, know him better as the father of NFL star QBs Peyton and Eli Manning.

FUNKY FACTS

→ Yes, the Saints were bad ... for a long time. During some of their worst stretches, fans wore paper bags on their heads. They called the team the "Aints" (as in "they ain't that good!")

→ The first play in Saints history was a touchdown! John Gilliam returned the opening kickoff in 1967 for a score. Although the Saints lost, they did win three games in their first season.

→ Longtime Saints owner Tom Benson sometimes celebrated big wins by dancing on the sidelines with a Mardi Gras-style umbrella. Fans called it "The Benson Boogie."

SUPERSTAR:
DREW BREES

Since joining the Saints in 2006, Brees has become one of the NFL's best QBs. He threw for 5,069 yards in 2008, the second-highest total ever and one of three 4,000-yard-plus years for him in New Orleans.

→ One of the most popular Saints was QB Bobby Hebert (pronounced "eh-BEAR"). Many people in Louisiana are Cajuns, as is Hebert, so he was quite the local hero.

You Can Look It Up! NEW ORLEANS'S OFFICIAL WEBSITE: www.neworleanssaints.com

TAMPA BAY
BUCCANEERS

The Buccaneers are named for pirates; they have a pirate ship in their stadium and a pirate on their helmets. Arrrr! They've usually played like people defending against pirates, though, regularly boasting one of the NFL's best Ds.

GAME 1?
1976

The Buccaneers were born the year the United States turned 200. The team joined with fellow expansion club Seattle to bring the NFL up to a new total of 28 teams.

 ## MAGIC MOMENT
Super Bowl XXXVII

The Bucs' run of title-free seasons stopped here, with a 48–21 dismantling of the Raiders, making Tampa Bay 1–0 in Super Bowls!

 ## LOWEST LOW
Very Bad Start

They were not expected to do well, but this was wild. The 1976 Bucs became the first team to lose every game in a season, finishing 0–14.

STUFF

HOME:
Raymond James Stadium

SUPER BOWL TITLES: **1**

ONLY IN TAMPA:
A huge pirate ship "floats" behind one end zone. Cannons on the ship fire when the Bucs score.

STAR SEASONS!

1984 James Wilder had the best rushing season in team history, setting Bucs records with 13 touchdowns and 1,544 yards.

2001 Cornerback Ronde Barber led the NFL with ten interceptions.

2002 During the Bucs' Super Bowl season, Derrick Brooks became the first linebacker in NFL history to return three interceptions for TDs in a season.

The Ultimate Buc
DERRICK BROOKS

Talk about sticking with it: Linebacker Derrick Brooks started every Tampa Bay game from 1996–2008! He didn't just show up and play, though—he excelled. Brooks was the 2002 NFL Defensive Player of the Year and has been a 11-time Pro Bowl pick. He has made 25 interceptions and scored seven touchdowns!

FUNKY FACTS

➔ Until they switched to their current colors of dark red and gold in 1997, Tampa Bay wore some of the ugliest uniforms in the NFL. They were bright orange!

➔ Ronde Barber and his twin brother, former Giants star running back Tiki Barber, have written several books for kids about playing football when they were young.

➔ After QB Steve DeBerg threw a game-losing interception to Harry Carson of the Giants, Tampa coach John McKay said, "It would have

SUPERSTAR!
RONDE BARBER

In 12 seasons with Tampa Bay, Barber has established himself as one of the best cornerbacks in the NFL. Barber's 23 career sacks are a record for NFL cornerbacks. He's been selected for five Pro Bowls.

been a great pass if Harry was on our team."

➔ Defensive end Lee Roy Selmon (whose brother Dewey was also a Buc) was the first Tampa Bay player elected to the Hall of Fame. Lee Roy made the Hall in 1995.

You Can Look It Up! TAMPA BAY'S OFFICIAL WEB SITE: **www.buccaneers.com**

ARIZONA CARDINALS

The only people who saw the Cardinals' 2008 season coming were . . . well, no one. After a 60-year absence from the championship game, the Cardinals shocked the world by making it to the Super Bowl. What's next?

GAME 1?
1898

Founded as an athletic club, the Cardinals became one of the original NFL teams in 1920. They started in Chicago, moved to St. Louis in 1960, and then to Arizona in 1988.

 ## MAGIC MOMENT
Super Bowl XLIII

The Cardinals in the Super Bowl? It was a Cinderella run through the playoffs until the Steelers won in the last minute.

 ## LOWEST LOW
The Fallen Mighty

They were the NFL champions in 1947, but just a few years later, the Cardinals won only one game, finishing 1–10–1. Yuck.

STUFF

HOME:
University of Phoenix Stadium

SUPER BOWL TITLES: **0**

ONLY IN ARIZONA:
The Cards home has a retractable field! The surface rolls out of the stadium to let the grass bask in the sun.

STAR SEASONS!

2000 MarTay Jenkins set an all-time NFL record by returning 82 kickoffs for a total of 2,186 yards.

2005 Neil Rackers set an NFL record with 40 field goals, including six of seven from 50+ yards.

2008 Kurt Warner lit up the scoreboard for 30 touchdowns and 4,583 yards. It was his third season topping 4,000 yards.

The Ultimate Cardinal

JIM HART

Never a superstar, but always a steady, solid passer, Hart led the Cardinals for 15 seasons. He was the starting QB from 1967–1981 and a backup for two seasons after that. He's still the team's career leader in passing yards and touchdown passes. Not a Hall of Famer, but a high-flying Cardinal!

FUNKY FACTS

→ Ernie Nevers of the Chicago Cardinals set one of the NFL's oldest records in 1929. He scored six touchdowns and kicked four extra points for a still-standing single-game record of 40 points!

→ Why are the Cardinals called the Cardinals? In 1901, Chris O'Brien bought the club and ordered maroon uniforms. When they arrived, he said, "These aren't maroon. They're cardinal red!" The name stuck.

→ The kid turned out well: Cardinals superstar Larry Fitzgerald started

SUPERSTAR!

LARRY FITZGERALD

Known for having the best pair of hands in the NFL, Fitzgerald rose to new stardom in the 2008 playoffs. He set a record for the most receiving yards in a postseason with 546.

his football life as a ballboy with the Vikings in the 1990s.

→ Guard Conrad Dobler played for the Cardinals in the 1970s. He was known as "The Meanest Man in Football."

You Can Look It Up! ARIZONA'S OFFICIAL WEBSITE: www.azcardinals.com

ST. LOUIS
RAMS

The Rams have a long and proud history, filled with superstars at many positions. They have become an offensive powerhouse in recent years (though 2008 was a bit of a power outage!).

GAME 1?
1937

Rams fans have needed suitcases. The team started in 1937 in Cleveland. It moved to Los Angeles in 1946. In 1995, the Rams moved to St. Louis, the former home of the Cardinals.

 ## MAGIC MOMENT
Super Bowl XXXIV

The Rams held on to beat the Titans for their only Super Bowl title. Kurt Warner set a record with 414 passing yards.

 ## LOWEST LOW
Tough Stretch

The Rams have fallen on hard times, going a lamb-like 5–27 in 2007 and 2008. That's anything but "Ram tough."

STUFF

HOME:
Edward Jones Dome

SUPER BOWL TITLES: **1**

ONLY IN ST. LOUIS:
Now you see it, now you don't: The Jones Dome has a huge tray of "Magic Carpet" turf that rolls on and off the field.

STAR SEASONS!

1950
The Rams' big-play offense had one of its best seasons as Tom Fears led the NFL with 84 catches.

1984
Eric Dickerson set the single-season rushing record with 2,105 yards. He had set the rookie record with 1,808 the year before.

2001
QB Kurt Warner set a team record with 4,830 yards. He also passed for an NFL-best 36 TDs.

The Ultimate Ram

MERLIN OLSEN

No Rams player—in fact, no NFL player—has played in as many Pro Bowls (14) as defensive end Merlin Olsen. Quiet and thoughtful off the field, he was a terror on it, helping the 1960s–1970s Rams have one of the best D-lines ever. After his Hall-of-Fame career, he became an actor.

#1

FUNKY FACTS

→ Two were better than one! In the early 1950s, the Rams split the job of No. 1 quarterback. They had a pair of good ones—future Hall of Famers Bob Waterfield and Norm Van Brocklin.

→ The Rams defensive line in the 1960s had a very cool nickname: "The Fearsome Foursome." One of the group, Rosey Grier, seemed less fearsome later when he became an actor and a famous knitter.

→ In 1985, Rams QB Dieter Brock (a Canadian native) became the only man named Dieter in the history of the NFL.

SUPERSTAR!

STEVEN JACKSON

With his hair waving goodbye to trailing defenders, Jackson is one of the NFL's toughest runners. A four-time 1,000-yard rusher, Jackson is also a great receiver. He nabbed 90 catches in 2006.

→ Former team owner Georgia Frontiere was one of only a few women who have owned or run an NFL team. She took over the Rams after the death of her husband, Carroll Rosenbloom.

You Can Look It Up! ST. LOUIS'S OFFICIAL WEBSITE: www.stlouisrams.com

SAN FRANCISCO 49ERS

A long stretch of not-so-good, a decade of brilliance, and a recent past of, well . . . more not-so-good. Still, the 49ers have fielded some of the NFL's greatest players and won some of its most important games.

GAME 1?
1946

The Niners were part of the AAFC from 1946 to 1949. When the NFL gobbled that league up, the Niners were one of the teams that survived to join the "big" league in 1950.

 MAGIC MOMENT
The Catch

Joe Montana floated a pass late in the 1981 NFC title game. Dwight Clark soared and nabbed it. The 49ers dynasty was on!

 LOWEST LOW
Only Two?

Just two years after winning a division championship, the 49ers sank to an all-time low, finishing with a record of 2–14 in 2004.

STUFF

HOME:
Candlestick Park

SUPER BOWL TITLES: **5**

ONLY IN SAN FRANCISCO:
The team has had so many tough seasons before and after their dynasty years that their fans are called the "49er Faithful."

STAR SEASONS!

1954 Joe Perry became the last San Francisco player to lead the league in rushing.

1988 Running back Roger Craig led the NFL with 2,036 combined rushing and receiving yards and helped lead the Niners to their third Super Bowl win.

1995 Jerry Rice set an NFL record (one of dozens he owns) with 1,848 receiving yards in a season.

The Ultimate 49er

JOE MONTANA

When people make their lists of the "best quarterbacks of all time," Montana's name often ends up at the top. Thanks to his calm leadership and pinpoint passing, the 49ers won four Super Bowls in the 1980s, and Montana was the MVP in three of those wins. He was an easy choice for the Hall of Fame in 2000.

#1

FUNKY FACTS

➜ Hall-of-Fame QB Steve Young is the great-great-great grandson of Brigham Young, a famous leader of the Mormon religion in the 1800s. You can probably guess where Young played college football: Brigham Young University (natch!).

➜ Why 49ers? The team gets its name from the gold-crazed settlers who rushed to California in 1849.

➜ In the late 1950s, receiver R.C. Owens, who was a basketball star in college, perfected a play called the "Alley-Oop," in which he out-jumped a defender for the ball. The play was named for a popular cartoon character.

SUPERSTAR!

PATRICK WILLIS

After being named the best college linebacker in the country at the Univ. of Mississippi, Willis is on his way to becoming the best in the NFL. His field-spanning speed makes him a tackling machine!

➜ Tough-guy defensive back Ronnie Lott once had a choice: miss part of a season with an injured pinky, or have doctors cut off the tip of the finger so he could play. He played.

You Can Look It Up! SAN FRANCISCO'S OFFICIAL WEBSITE: www.49ers.com

SEATTLE
SEAHAWKS

The only NFL team in the Northwest has had a few bright moments, but it's never won the big prize. Several great players have worn the Seahawks blue and green, but none of them have worn a Super Bowl ring . . . yet.

GAME 1?
1976

The Seahawks were an expansion team in 1976. They played their first season in the NFC, moved to the AFC through 2001, and shifted back to the NFC West in 2002.

MAGIC MOMENT
Super Bowl XL

The Seahawks earned their first NFC title in 2005 and headed to their first (and only) Super Bowl, where they lost to Pittsburgh.

LOWEST LOW
No Pop!

Seattle scored only 140 points in 16 games in 1992. Not surprisingly, they won only twice and had their worst season ever.

STUFF

HOME:
Qwest Field

SUPER BOWL TITLES: 0

ONLY IN SEATTLE:
Seattle fans can take their boats across the water to a dock near the stadium. Then they walk from the dock to their seats!

STAR SEASONS!

1998 Michael Sinclair led the NFL with 16.5 sacks. The defensive end earned his third Pro Bowl selection, too.

2005 Shaun Alexander led the NFL with 1,880 rushing yards and set a new single-season record (since broken) with 28 touchdowns.

2007 QB Matt Hasselbeck set a team record with 3,966 passing yards. He also threw 28 TDs.

The Ultimate Seahawk
STEVE LARGENT

Sticky-fingered Steve Largent was the NFL's all-time leader in TD catches (100) and receptions (819) when he retired in 1989. Largent was not the biggest receiver in the game, but he always seemed to be open for Seattle QBs. The Hall of Famer joined another team in 1994 when he was elected to Congress.

FUNKY FACTS

➜ What's a seahawk? That's actually a nickname for a bird called an osprey. With Seattle located on Puget Sound near the Pacific Ocean, seabirds are often seen in the area.

➜ It was kind of a joke, but when he was the Seahawks QB coach, Jim Zorn used a watery Slip 'n' Slide to help his QBs learn to slide.

➜ The Seahawks have retired the number 12 in honor of their fans. Football teams sometimes call their fans the "12th man," since their cheering helps the real 11 players do their best!

SUPERSTAR!
WALTER JONES

Jones has been to more Pro Bowls than any Seattle player—nine! The offensive tackle's powerful blocking opens holes for Seattle's runners and keeps his quarterback's jersey nice and clean.

➜ Dave Krieg was sacked a record seven times by Kansas City's Derrick Thomas in a game in 1990. But Krieg eluded Thomas's grasp on the last play and threw the winning touchdown pass as time ran out.

You Can Look It Up! SEATTLE'S OFFICIAL WEBSITE: www.seahawks.com

NFL RULES!

The NFL rule book is more than 100 pages long. Officials and coaches read it at bedtime like you read adventure stories. The rules range from the obvious (a field goal has to go above the crossbar) to the obscure (no blocking a defender below the knees if another player is blocking him above the waist at the same time). Here are a few pages with some of the basic, some of the odd, and a few of the cool facts about NFL rules.

Some Basics

▶▶NFL teams can have no more than 11 players on the field for a play.

▶▶One team wears a colored jersey; the other team wears a white jersey. (The league makes some exceptions, such as for old-time "throwback" jerseys.)

▶▶The teams must use official NFL footballs (no Nerfs!).

▶▶The offense must move at least ten yards in four plays (or "downs"). If it fails to gain ten yards, the other team takes possession of the ball.

▶▶The teams play four 15-minute quarters—60 minutes of time on the game clock.

▶▶There are numerous rules for where each offensive player can line up, who can move, and when he can move to before a play starts.

▶▶For a touchdown, the ball must "break the plane" of the goal line, which means it only has to barely get into the end zone. A field goal must go over the crossbar and between the goalposts.

SCORING CHART

How many points are scores worth? Believe it or not, that has changed over the years. Here's how they've changed and when.

SCORE	TODAY	BEFORE	BEFORE THAT!
Touchdown	6 (1912)	5 (1898)	4 (1876)
Field goal	3 (1909)	4 (1904)	5 (1876)
PAT*	1 or 2 (1994)	1 only (1876)	

*Point after touchdown.

MOST MISUNDERSTOOD RULES

Interference When covering a receiver, a defender can't make contact with that receiver once he's five yards past the line of scrimmage. If he does before the ball is thrown, it's called illegal contact. That's a five-yard penalty and an automatic first down for the offense. If he hits, pulls, pushes, or gets in the way of the receiver while the ball is in the air, that's interference. The ball is placed at the spot of the foul, so it can be a big penalty (and it's an automatic first down). Offensive players can also be called for interference against a defender, but not for illegal contact.

Offside/Encroachment/False Start *Offside* is when a defender is beyond the line of scrimmage when the ball is snapped, but he has not made contact with the offense. It's *encroachment* if he makes contact with an offensive player before the ball is snapped. A *false start* is when an offensive player moves from a set position before the snap of the ball. (Any player on the offense can be called for this, not just linemen.)

Was It a Catch? NFL officials often have to rule whether a player has made a legal catch. For it to be a catch, the player has to have both feet (or his body or one knee) land inbounds while he is in control of the football. The football should not touch the ground. If a player catches the ball in the air, but does not keep control of the ball as he lands, it's not a catch. It's also not a catch if he lands out of bounds. (In college, a player needs only one foot inbounds to make a catch.)

UNUSUAL RULES

Most of the rules in the NFL are pretty well known. No punching a guy in the face. No spitting. Don't eat the football, etc. Other rules don't come up that often. But they're still rules! Impress your friends by knowing these NFL tidbits.

Leave the Holder Alone
Everyone knows that running into the kicker or punter after a kick is against the rules. Did you know it's also a penalty to run into the holder after field goals and extra points?

Watch That Pass!
A quarterback swings a pass out to a running back, who stands a few yards behind and to the side. The back drops the pass. Incompletion, right? Nope, it's a fumble—a missed lateral—and it's a live ball! Defenders, make sure you pick it up and run!

Free Kicks
You know that teams receive a free kick after they score a safety. Did you know that they can also get another type of free kick after a fair catch? A team can try a field goal—with no blockers—from the spot of any fair catch. The Packers tried it in 2008, just missing a 69-yard field goal try!

RULES QUIZ

See how well you know these NFL rules. Answers are upside down below.

1. Which of these is not the name of a penalty? encroachment; illegal shift; rudeness.

2. True or false: Players can finish a play even if their helmet flies off.

3. Each quarter of an NFL game is: 10 minutes; 12 minutes; 15 minutes.

4. The "neutral zone" is: in outer space; along the line of scrimmage; in a quarterback's head.

5. A referee puts his hands together over his head. What is he signaling?

Answers: 1. rudeness; 2. true; 3. 15 minutes; 4. along the line of scrimmage; 5. a safety

FIND OUT MORE

This is the *Scholastic Ultimate Guide to Football*, but believe it or not, there's even more out there about the grand old game of football. Check out these books and websites to satisfy all your football needs.

BOOKS

EYEWITNESS: FOOTBALL
By James Buckley, Jr. *(hey, that's me!)*
(DK, 1999)
Check out all the gear, history, trophies, and memories from 80-plus NFL seasons. Packed with color photos!

HEROES OF FOOTBALL
By John Madden and Bill Gutman
(Dutton, 2006)
The famous coach/video-game dude takes you through the entire history of pro football.

PLAY FOOTBALL!
By Tim Polzer
(DK, 2003)
Wanna play the game? This official NFL book gives you tips on every skill and position, plus advice from NFL stars.

WEBSITES

www.nfl.com
This is your one-stop shopping extravaganza for stats, videos, stories, and player bios.

www.nflrush.com
This special "for kids only" site features player interviews, playing tips, and games.

www.TEAMNAME.com
Don't type in "TEAMNAME." Type in your favorite NFL team's name and find their official site, with all the details of your fave players.

GLOSSARY

appendix a tiny part of a human's intestine that can be removed if it becomes infected

benchmark a performance, such as 1,000 yards in a season, that's used to judge the performance of others

Cajun a person from Louisiana who is descended from French-speaking immigrants from Nova Scotia, a province in Canada

defunct no longer in operation

equipment manager person on a sports team who takes care of all the team's gear

expansion team a team that is added to an existing sports league

high-impact able to withstand heavy blows or pressure

innovator an inventor or creator

irrelevant something that doesn't matter or have any importance

lateral in football, a pass that goes backward

obscure rare, unusual, not widely known

permutation one possible outcome of a situation

ricochet when an object bounces off another

rituals actions that are carried out in the same way each time

rout complete destruction; in sports, a win by many points

schnozzes a slang term for noses

spur to encourage someone to act

ultimate greatest or best

INDEX

OVERTIME!

We're having so much fun, we couldn't stop! Here's another page of NFL facts, all about overtime! Since 1974, NFL games that are tied after four quarters go to a quarter of sudden-death overtime. Sudden-death means that the first team to score wins. If no one scores in the bonus quarter, the game remains a tie (in the regular season only). Here are some memorable overtime games.

Over in an Instant I
The shortest overtime game was in 2002. Facing the Bills, the Jets' Chad Morton returned the opening kickoff 96 yards. Game over! What the two teams couldn't resolve in 60 minutes, Morton resolved in only 14 seconds.

Over in an Instant II
On the first play from scrimmage in a 2007 overtime game, Green Bay's Brett Favre hit Greg Jennings with an 82-yard TD bomb! The overtime took only 16 seconds, the second-shortest ever.

Brown Back-to-Back
In 2001, Chicago cornerback Mike Brown returned interceptions to win overtime contests—in back-to-back games! The Bears beat the Browns and 49ers via this "Brown-out."

Go Really, Really Long!
In a 1985 game, the Eagles' Ron Jaworski hit Mike Quick with what turned into a 99-yard TD pass play, giving Philly a win over Atlanta.

Kicker Turned Runner
In a 1980 game, Packers kicker Chester Marcol had a potential game-winning field goal blocked. No problem. Marcol picked up the bouncing ball and ran for a touchdown instead!

BONUS
Denver has won the most overtimes games: 21. Miami and New England have each lost the most OT games: 18. And just hope you don't face the Ravens in the "fifth" quarter. They have the highest OT winning percentage among teams with at least ten such wins: .654.